Ready, Set, Go!

Trigonometry

Workbook

Mel Friedman, M.S.

Research & Education Association
Visit our website at
www.rea.com

Research & Education Association

61 Ethel Road West
Piscataway, New Jersey 08854
E-mail: info@rea.com

***REA's Ready, Set, Go!*™**
Trigonometry Workbook

Printed in the United States of America

ISBN-13: 978-0-7386-0455-8
ISBN-10: 0-7386-0455-0

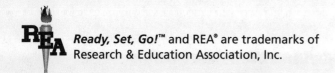

Ready, Set, Go!™ and REA® are trademarks of
Research & Education Association, Inc.

Contents

Welcome

to the *Ready, Set, Go!* Trigonometry Workbook!

About This Book

This book will help high school math students at all learning levels understand basic trigonometry. Students will develop the skills, confidence, and knowledge they need to succeed on high school math exams with emphasis on passing high school graduation exams.

Fifteen easy-to-follow lessons break down the material into the basics. In-depth, step-by-step examples and solutions reinforce student learning, while the "Math Flash" feature provides useful tips and strategies, including advice on common mistakes to avoid.

Students can take drills and quizzes to test themselves on the subject matter, then review any areas in which they need improvement or additional reinforcement. The book concludes with a final exam, designed to comprehensively test what students have learned.

The *Ready, Set, Go! Trigonometry Workbook* will help students master the basics of mathematics—and help them face their next math test—with confidence!

Icons Explained

Icons make navigating through the book easier. The icons, explained below, highlight tips and strategies, where to review a topic, and the drills found at the end of each lesson.

Look for the **"Math Flash"** feature for helpful tips and strategies, including advice on how to avoid common mistakes.

When you see the **"Let's Review"** icon, you know just where to look for more help with the topic on which you are currently working.

The **"Test Yourself!"** icon, found at the end of every lesson, signals a short drill that reviews the skills you have studied in that lesson.

To the Student

This workbook will help you master the fundamentals of trigonometry. It offers you the support you need to boost your skills and helps you succeed in school and beyond!

It takes the guesswork out of math by explaining what you most need to know in a step-by-step format. When you apply what you learn from this workbook, you can

1. do better in class;

2. raise your grades, and

3. score higher on your high school math exams.

Each compact lesson in this book introduces a math concept and explains the method behind it in plain language. This is followed with lots of examples with fully worked-out solutions that take you through the key points of each problem.

The book gives you two tools to measure what you learn along the way:

✔ Short drills that follow <u>each</u> lesson

✔ Quizzes that test you on <u>multiple</u> lessons

These tools are designed to comfortably build your test-taking confidence.

Meanwhile, the "Math Flash" feature throughout the book offers helpful tips and strategies—including advice on how to avoid common mistakes.

When you complete the lessons, take the final exam at the end of the workbook to see how far you've come. If you still need to strengthen your grasp on any concept, you can always go back to the related lesson and review at your own pace.

To the Parent

For many students, math can be a challenge—but with the right tools and support, your child can master the basics of trigonometry. As educational publishers, our goal is to help all students develop the crucial math skills they'll need in school and beyond.

This *Ready, Set, Go! Workbook* is intended for students who need to build their basic trigonometry skills. It was specifically created and designed to assist students who need a boost in understanding and learning the math concepts that are most tested along the path to graduation. Through a series of easy-to-follow lessons, students are introduced to the essential mathematical ideas and methods, and then take short quizzes to test what they are learning.

Each lesson is devoted to a key mathematical building block. The concepts and methods are fully explained, then reinforced with examples and detailed solutions. Your child will be able to test what he or she has learned along the way, and then take a cumulative exam found at the end of the book.

Whether used in school with teachers, for home study, or with a tutor, the ***Ready, Set, Go! Workbook*** is a great support tool. It can help improve your child's math proficiency in a way that's fun and educational!

To the Teacher

As you know, not all students learn the same, or at the same pace. And most students require additional instruction, guidance, and support in order to do well academically.

Using the Curriculum Focal Points of the National Council of Teachers of Mathematics, this workbook was created to help students increase their math abilities and succeed on high school exams with special emphasis on high school proficiency exams. The book's easy-to-follow lessons offer a review of the basic material, supported by examples and detailed solutions that illustrate and reinforce what the students have learned.

To accommodate different pacing for students, we provide drills and quizzes throughout the book to enable students to mark their progress. This approach allows for the mastery of smaller chunks of material and provides a greater opportunity to build mathematical competence and confidence.

When we field-tested this series in the classroom, we made every effort to ensure that the book would accommodate the common need to build basic math skills as effectively and flexibly as possible. Therefore, this book can be used in conjunction with lesson plans, stand alone as a single teaching source, or be used in a group-learning environment. The practice quizzes and drills can be given in the classroom as part of the overall curriculum or used for independent study. A cumulative exam at the end of the workbook helps students (and their instructors) gauge their mastery of the subject matter.

We are confident that this workbook will help your students develop the necessary skills and build the confidence they need to succeed on high school math exams.

About Research & Education Association

Founded in 1959, Research & Education Association (REA) is dedicated to publishing the finest and most effective educational materials—including software, study guides, and test preps—for students in elementary school, middle school, high school, college, graduate school, and beyond.

Today, REA's wide-ranging catalog is a leading resource for teachers, students, and professionals.

We invite you to visit us at *www.rea.com* to find out how "REA is making the world smarter."

About the Author

Author Mel Friedman is a former classroom teacher and test-item writer for Educational Testing Service and ACT, Inc.

Acknowledgments

We would like to thank Larry Kling, Vice President, Editorial, for his editorial direction; Pam Weston, Vice President, Publishing, for setting the quality standards for production integrity and managing the publication to completion; Alice Leonard, Senior Editor, for project management and preflight editorial review; Diane Goldschmidt, Senior Editor, for post-production quality assurance; Rachel DiMatteo, Graphic Artist, for page design; Christine Saul, Senior Graphic Artist, for cover design; and Jeff LoBalbo, Senior Graphic Artist, for post-production file mapping.

We also gratefully acknowledge Heather Brashear for copyediting, and Kathy Caratozzolo of Caragraphics for typesetting.

A special thank you to Orsolina Cetta of Piscataway High School, Piscataway, NJ, and to Tracy Doherty and Mary Willi of Union Catholic High School, Scotch Plains, NJ, for their technical review of the lessons and tests in this book.

Graphs of Points and Angles

Trigonometry is defined as the branch of mathematics that deals primarily with the relationship that exists between the sides and angles of a triangle. However, you will also discover other applications. In this lesson, you will be introduced to **plotting points** and the **measures of angles on the *xy*-coordinate system**. For this lesson, angle measures will not exceed 360°.

Your Goal: When you have completed this lesson, you should be able to determine the measure of an angle, as well as classify angles into categories. You will also be able to convert angles from one system of measurement to another.

LESSON 1

Graphs of Points and Angles

The **xy-coordinate system** is also known as the **rectangular coordinate system** or the **Cartesian coordinate system**. We start with a flat surface, which is known as a **plane**. Then, we draw two number lines that are perpendicular to each other and that intersect at the number zero. The horizontal line is labeled the *x*-axis, and the vertical line is labeled the *y*-axis.

On the **x-axis**, all positive numbers lie to the right of the intersection point and all negative numbers lie to the left. On the **y-axis**, all positive numbers lie above the intersection point and all negative numbers lie below. For consistency, the numbers are evenly spaced. Figure 1.1 shows the *xy*-coordinate system with this information.

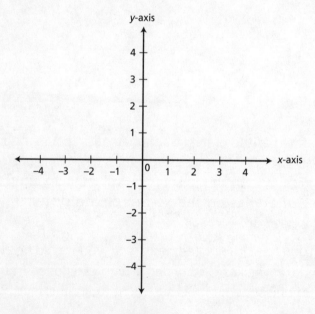

Figure 1.1

*Even though the only numbers shown for each axis are –4 through +4, be aware that each **axis represents a real number line**. This means that these lines include numbers that are less than –4, greater than +4, as well as fractions, decimals, and square roots.*

Notice that the *x*-axis and *y*-axis divide the plane into <u>four regions</u>, each of which is called a **quadrant.** These quadrants are numbered using Roman numerals I, II, III, and IV (instead of 1, 2, 3, and 4). The numbering begins in the upper right quadrant, continues in a counterclockwise direction, and ends in the lower right quadrant. Figure 1.2 illustrates this numbering system.

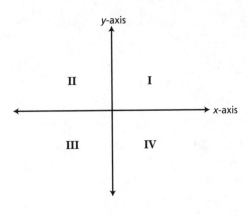

Figure 1.2

Each point on this plane is assigned a corresponding *x* value and a corresponding *y* value, which will be written in the form (*x, y*). The expression (*x, y*) is called the **ordered pair** for the corresponding point. Each of *x* and *y* is called a **coordinate** of the ordered pair. The point where the two axes intersect is labeled (0, 0) and is called the **origin**.

Suppose point *A* is located 2 units to the right and 3 units above (0, 0). Then (2, 3) is the ordered pair for point *A*. Any point in the first quadrant will always be assigned an ordered pair in which each of *x* and *y* is positive.

Suppose point *B* is located 1 unit to the left and 4 units above (0, 0). Then (–1, 4) is the ordered pair for point *B*. Any point in the second quadrant will always be assigned an ordered pair in which *x* is negative and *y* is positive.

Suppose point *C* is located 3 units to the left and 5 units down from (0, 0). Then (–3, –5) is the ordered pair for point *C*. Any point in the third quadrant will always be assigned an ordered pair in which each of *x* and *y* is negative.

Suppose point *D* is located 4 units to the right and 2 units down from (0, 0). Then (4, –2) is the ordered pair for point *D*. Any point in the fourth quadrant will always be assigned an ordered pair in which *x* is positive and *y* is negative. Figure 1.3 shows points *A, B, C,* and *D*.

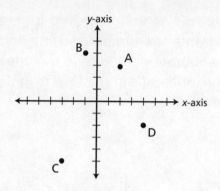

Figure 1.3

Now consider point *E*, which is located 5 units directly to the right of (0, 0). Then (5, 0) is the ordered pair for point *E*. Notice that *E* lies on the positive portion of the *x*-axis. If point *F* is located 4 units above (0, 0), then its corresponding ordered pair is (0, 4). Notice that *F* lies on the positive portion of the *y*-axis.

Similarly, if point *G* lies 2 units to the left of (0, 0), then its location is given by (–2, 0). Finally, if point *H* lies 1 unit below (0, 0), then its location is given by (0, –1). Figure 1.4 shows points *E*, *F*, *G*, and *H*.

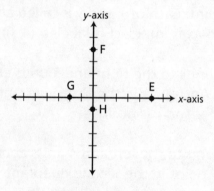

Figure 1.4

MathFlash!

None of points *E, F, G,* or *H* is considered to *lie in any quadrant,* because they lie on either the *x*-axis or the *y*-axis.

An **angle** is composed of two rays with a common endpoint, called a **vertex**. The common ways in which an angle is named are by

(a)   the letter representing its vertex, or

(b)   three letters in which the middle letter represents the vertex and each of the other two letters represents a point on each ray. The symbol for angle is $\angle$.

Figure 1.5, shows the three ways to name the given angle: $\angle JKM$, $\angle MKJ$, and $\angle K$.

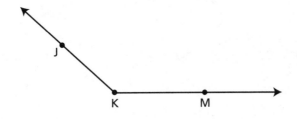

Figure 1.5

The same symbol $\angle$ is used regardless of the actual size of the angle.

Angles are most commonly measured in **degrees**. A degree represents an opening that is exactly $\frac{1}{360}$ th of a complete rotation of a ray around a point. Figure 1.6 shows angle *R*, whose measure is 1°. This is written as $m\angle R = 1°$.

Figure 1.6

Angles are classified according to their sizes.

- An **acute** angle is one whose measure is more than 0°, but less than 90°.

- A **right** angle is one whose measure is exactly 90°.

- An **obtuse** angle is one whose measure is greater than 90°, but less than 180°.

- A **straight** angle is one whose measure is exactly 180°.

- A **reflex** angle is one whose measure is greater than 180°, but less than 360°.

Figures 1.7 through 1.11 show each of these types of angles, where the *curve* (⌒) shows the part of the angle being measured. Note that a small box is used to designate a 90° angle.

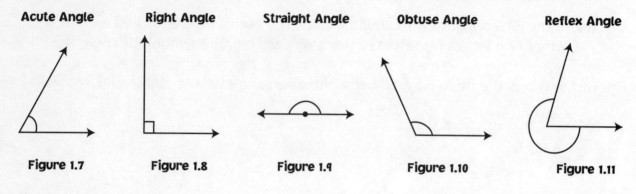

Acute Angle	Right Angle	Straight Angle	Obtuse Angle	Reflex Angle
Figure 1.7	Figure 1.8	Figure 1.9	Figure 1.10	Figure 1.11

MathFlash!

The direction in which the rays face does <u>not</u> affect the measures of the angles.

In addition to degrees, another common way to measure angles is **radians**. One radian is an angle measure in which the intercepted arc length equals the length of the radius. Suppose a circle is given in which a central angle intercepts an arc of the circle whose length is exactly equal to the length of the radius. Figure 1.12 illustrates this concept.

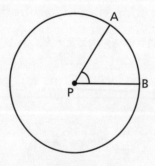

Figure 1.12

In this circle, point P is the center. The length of $\overset{\frown}{AB}$ is equal to the length of each of $\overline{PA}$ and $\overline{PB}$, since they are both radii. The measure of $\angle APB$ is 1 radian. In order to convert 1 radian to a measurement in degrees, we use the formula for the circumference of a circle: $C = 2\pi r$, where r is the length of the radius. We know that r is the length of $\overset{\frown}{AB}$ and that 360° corresponds to the circumference.

Let x represent the number of degrees in $\overset{\frown}{AB}$.

Using a proportion, we can write $\dfrac{x}{360} = \dfrac{r}{2\pi r}$.

Canceling out the r's, we get $\dfrac{x}{360} = \dfrac{1}{2\pi}$.

Cross multiplying leads to $2\pi x = 360$, so $x = \dfrac{360}{2\pi} = \dfrac{180}{\pi}$ degrees.

Using 3.14 as the approximate value of π, $\dfrac{180}{\pi} \approx 57.3°$.

Now if 1 radian is $\dfrac{180}{\pi}$ degrees, we can also convert 1 degree into radians.

Using the equation 1 radian $= \dfrac{180}{\pi}$ degrees, multiply both sides by $\dfrac{\pi}{180}$.

The equation becomes $\left(\dfrac{\pi}{180}\right)(1 \text{ radian}) = \left(\dfrac{\pi}{180}\right)\left(\dfrac{180}{\pi}\right)$ degrees.

Simplifying, we get $\dfrac{\pi}{180}$ radians = 1 degree.

Using 3.14 as the approximate value of π, we can see that 1 degree ≈ 0.017 radians.

Here are the rules to follow for conversion from degrees to radians or vice versa:

To change from degrees to radians, multiply by $\dfrac{\pi}{180}$ and insert "radians."

To change from radians to degrees, multiply by $\dfrac{180}{\pi}$ and insert "degrees."

MathFlash!

We will use "rad" as the abbreviation for "radians" and the symbol "°" as the abbreviation for "degrees."

Let's review the material in this introductory lesson with some examples.
<u>For Examples 1, 2, and 3</u>, use the *xy*-coordinate system shown below.

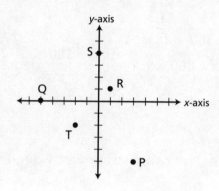

1   **Example:**   *What are the coordinates of point P?*

Solution: Point *P* lies 3 units to the right and 5 units down from (0, 0).
Thus, its coordinates are (3, –5).

2   **Example:**   *Which points do not lie in any quadrant?*

Solution: The coordinates of point *Q* are (–5, 0). This point is on the *x*-axis;
therefore, it does not lie in any quadrant. The coordinates of point
S are (0, 4). Since this point is on the *y*-axis, it also does not lie in
any quadrant.

3   **Example:**   *Point T lies in which quadrant?*

Solution: Since the *x*- and *y*-coordinates of point *T* are negative, it must lie in
the third quadrant.

4 **Example:**   *Consider the following angle.*

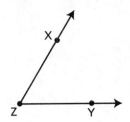

Which one of the following is not a correct way to name this angle?

(A) ∠Z   (C) ∠XZY

(B) ∠YXZ   (D) ∠YZX

Solution: The correct answer is (B). One way to name an angle is to use its vertex, which is Z. Another way is to use three letters, in which the middle letter is the vertex and the other letters represent points on each of the two rays that form the angle. (A), (C), and (D) correctly name this angle.

If you were asked to identify the type of angle shown in Example 4, there would be two possible answers. It would be an acute angle if it were marked as

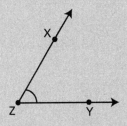

However, it would be a reflex angle if it were marked as

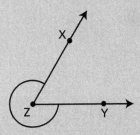

5 **Example:**   *What is the name of the following angle?*

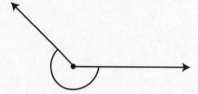

Answer: _____

Solution: Since the angle measure is greater than 180° but less than 360°, it is called a reflex angle.

6 **Example:**   *Which one of the following is a measure of an obtuse angle?*

(A) *90°*   (C) *195°*

(B) *75°*   (D) *175°*

Solution: The correct answer is (D). An obtuse angle must have a measurement greater than 90° but less than 180°.

7 **Example:**   *How many radians are equivalent to 60°?*

Solution: To convert from degrees to radians, multiply by $\frac{\pi}{180}$. Thus, 60° is equivalent to $(60)\left(\frac{\pi}{180}\right) = \frac{\pi}{3}$ rad.

MathFlash!

Looking at the solution to Example 7, unless the instructions ask for an approximate answer, you should leave your answer in "π" form. Had the instructions said to provide an approximation, an acceptable answer would be 1.05.

8 Example: *How many degrees are equivalent to $\frac{7\pi}{8}$ radians?*

Solution: To convert from radians to degrees, multiply by $\frac{180}{\pi}$. Thus, $\frac{7\pi}{8}$ rad is equivalent to $\left(\frac{7\pi}{8}\right)\left(\frac{180}{\pi}\right)$ degrees. Cancel out π's. Also, since 4 is a common factor of 8 and 180, change 8 to 2 and change 180 to 45. The answer becomes $\left(\frac{7}{2}\right)\left(\frac{45}{1}\right) = 157.5°$.

9 Example: *When the hour hand of a watch moves from the number 12 to the number 4, through how many degrees does it rotate?*

Solution: The hour hand rotates through 4 numbers. Since a rotation of 12 numbers represents 360°, the answer is $\left(\frac{4}{12}\right)(360) = 120°$.

10 Example: *When the minute hand of a clock moves from the number 5 to the number 6, through how many radians does it rotate?*

Solution: The minute hand rotates through 1 number in going from 5 to 6. A rotation of 12 numbers represents 360°, which is equivalent to 2π radians. Thus, the answer is $\left(\frac{1}{12}\right)(2\pi) = \frac{\pi}{6}$ rad.

Test Yourself!

1. How many degrees are equivalent to $\frac{6\pi}{5}$ radians?   Answer: _____

2. How many degrees are there in a straight angle?   Answer: _____

3. Which one of the following points is located in quadrant II?

    (A) (–9, 0)   (C) (–7, 4)

    (B) (8, –2)   (D) (–5, –1)

4. If a point is not located in any quadrant, which one of the following is correct?

(A) At least one of its *x*- or *y*-coordinates must be zero.

(B) Both its *x*- and *y*-coordinates must be zero.

(C) Neither of its *x*- or *y*-coordinates is zero.

(D) Its *x*-coordinate must be zero, and its *y*-coordinate must not be zero.

5. How many radians are equivalent to 135°?   *Answer:* _____

6. Which one of the following is a correct representation of a reflex angle?

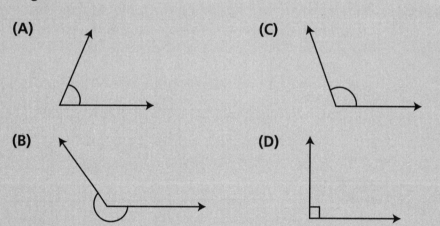

7. When the hour hand of a clock moves from the number 3 to the number 8, through how many degrees does it rotate?

Answer: _____

Test Yourself! (continued)

8.   **Consider the following angle.**

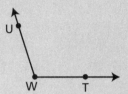

Which one of the following is <u>not</u> a correct way to name this angle?

(A)   ∠TWU   (C)   ∠TUW

(B)   ∠UWT   (D)   ∠W

9.   **To the nearest tenth of a degree, how many degrees would be equivalent to 3 radians?**

Answer: _____

10.   **When the minute hand of a watch moves from the number 1 to the number 10, through how many radians does it rotate?**

Answer: _____

Basics of Trigonometric Ratios—Part I

In this lesson, we will explore the method in which angles are measured in the *xy*-coordinate plane. We will introduce one of six trigonometric terms that together will form the **foundation of all our remaining lessons** in this book. As in Lesson 1, angle measures will not exceed 360°.

Your Goal: When you have completed this lesson, you should be able to determine the measure of an angle when it is shown on the *xy*-coordinate plane. You will also understand how one of the trigonometric terms is related to the sides of a triangle.

LESSON 2

Basics of Trigonometric Ratios—Part I

An angle is considered to be in **standard position** if its vertex is located at (0, 0) of the *xy*-coordinate system and its **initial** ray is the positive *x*-axis. The other ray of the angle is called its **terminal** ray. The position of the terminal ray determines the quadrant in which the angle lies. If the terminal ray coincides with the *x*- or *y*-axis, the angle is called a **quadrantal** angle. The **Greek letter θ**, pronounced "thay'-tuh," is commonly used when referring to an angle in standard position. Other Greek letters will also be used to represent angles.

If the direction in which the angle is measured is counterclockwise, the angle measure is considered <u>positive</u>. If the direction in which the angle is measured is clockwise, the angle measure is considered <u>negative</u>. The actual direction will be shown with a curved arrow.

For this lesson, all angles will be measured in a counterclockwise direction. Figures 2.1 through 2.6 are examples of angles in standard position and their associated quadrants.

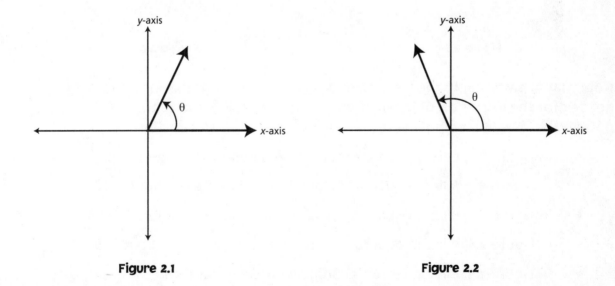

Figure 2.1   Figure 2.2

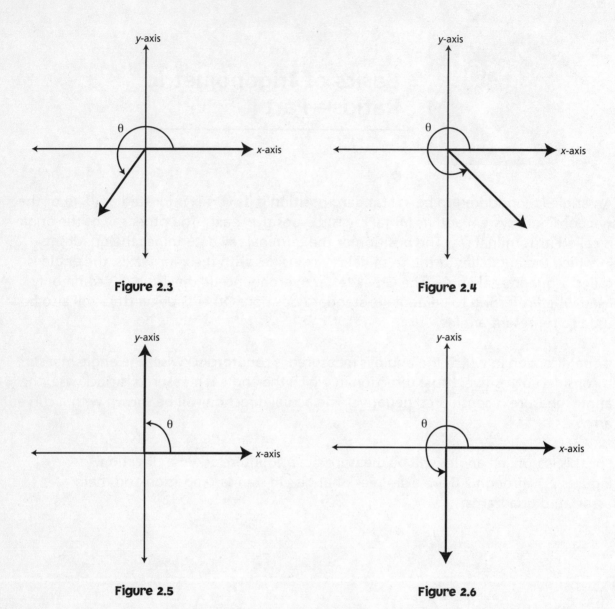

Figure 2.3

Figure 2.4

Figure 2.5

Figure 2.6

Note that in each graph, the scale markings have been omitted, since they are not needed for the discussion of labeling angles. The symbol ⤹ shows that each angle is positive, because it is being measured in a counterclockwise direction.

- In Figure 2.1, θ lies in quadrant I and has a measure of about 60°.

- In Figure 2.2, θ lies in quadrant II and has a measure of about 115°.

- In Figure 2.3, θ lies in quadrant III and has a measure of about 230°.

- In Figure 2.4, θ lies in quadrant IV and has a measure of about 315°.

- In Figure 2.5, θ is a quadrantal angle whose measure is 90°.

- In Figure 2.6, θ is a quadrantal angle whose measure is 270°.

Angles can be measured in radians. Based on the above discussion, angle measures of 0 radians, $\frac{\pi}{2}$ radians, π radians, $\frac{3\pi}{2}$ radians, and 2π radians all represent quadrantal angles.

Let's now use an angle θ that lies in quadrant I and draw a right triangle *OAP*, as shown in Figure 2.7, with a right angle at point *A*. Point *O* is the origin, and its coordinates are (0, 0).

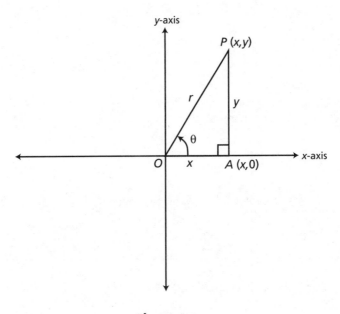

Figure 2.7

Let *x* represent the distance along the *x*-axis from the origin to point *A*.
Thus, the coordinates of point *A* are (*x*, 0).
Let *y* represent the vertical distance from point *A* to point *P*.
Thus, the coordinates of point *P* are (*x*, *y*).
Let *r* represent the distance from the origin to point *P*.

Then **sine θ**, read as "the sine of theta," is defined to be the ratio of the length of the opposite side of this triangle to the length of the hypotenuse. In this figure, *y* represents the length of the opposite side, and *r* represents the length of the hypotenuse. Since sine θ is often abbreviated as sin θ, we can write $\sin \theta = \frac{y}{r}$.

You may be wondering if given a particular value of θ, where θ lies in the first quadrant, does sin θ have only one particular value. The answer is an emphatic "yes."

Figures 2.8, 2.9, and 2.10 show three triangles drawn with the same angle θ in the first quadrant. For these triangles, each of θ_1, θ_2, and $\theta_3 = 30°$.

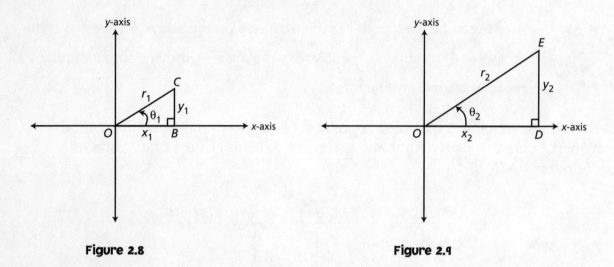

Figure 2.8   **Figure 2.9**

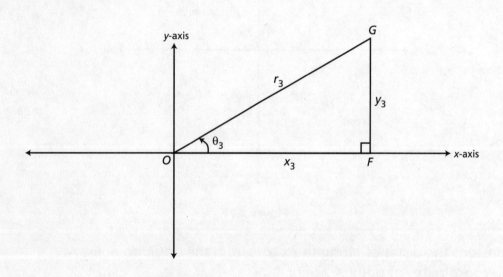

Figure 2.10

In geometry you learned that each one of triangles *OBC, ODE,* and *OFG* is similar to each of the other two triangles. For similar triangles, each pair of corresponding angles are congruent, and their corresponding sides must be in proportion. In particular, for Figures 2.8, 2.9, and 2.10, $\dfrac{y_1}{r_1} = \dfrac{y_2}{r_2} = \dfrac{y_3}{r_3}$.

Recall that we are using 30° as the measure of each of the angles θ_1, θ_2, and θ_3.
Using a ruler, measure each of the sides y_1, r_1, y_2, r_2, y_3, r_3.
Try to determine the relationship between *y* and *r*.
You should find that $r_1 = 2y_1$, $r_2 = 2y_2$, and $r_3 = 2y_3$.

Another way to express these three equations is $\dfrac{y_1}{r_1} = \dfrac{y_2}{r_2} = \dfrac{y_3}{r_3} = \dfrac{1}{2}$.

Thus, we can write $\sin 30° = \dfrac{1}{2}$.

Nearly every calculator has trigonometric functions capability. If you press the button marked *sin*, then press the number *30*, and then press the =, the calculator should read 0.5 or just .5, which of course is $\dfrac{1}{2}$.

The good news is that you don't have to measure the ratio of *y* to *r* for any right triangle drawn in the first quadrant. Regardless of the size of the angle θ, pressing the *sin* button for the angle measure will reveal the ratio of *y* to *r*.

Caution: When using degrees to measure angles, be sure that your calculator is in "degree" mode before you press the *sin 30*.

MathFlash!

The ratio of y to r is also referred to as the ratio of the opposite side to the hypotenuse of a right triangle. We can write
$$\sin \theta = \frac{opposite\ side}{hypotenuse}$$ *to express the meaning of the sine of θ.*

Figure 2.11 is another graphic illustration of the meaning of the sine of an acute angle.

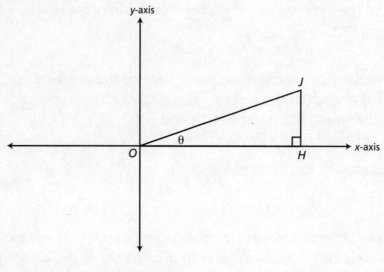

Figure 2.11

For ΔOHJ, the right angle is at H and θ = 19°. We need not draw three triangles with the same angle measurement at point O, as we did in Figures 2.8, 2.9, and 2.10. (We already know that the three triangles would be similar.)

Use your ruler to measure y (HJ) and r (OJ), to determine a relationship between y and r. If you are guessing that r appears to be about 3 times the size of y, then you are right on target! This would imply that sin 19° ≈ $\frac{1}{3}$. Sure enough, if you press sin 19°, the calculator will read approximately 0.3256. This is very close to the value of $\frac{1}{3}$, which is 0.333333... .

You can use your calculator to find the sine value ratios for any acute angle. These ratios will read as decimal numbers. Since the angles are in standard position, we really don't even need to draw the triangles on an *xy*-coordinate plane. In fact, if the triangle is not drawn with an angle in standard position, we can simply "reposition" it.

1   **Example:**   *What is the value of sin 25° to the nearest ten-thousandth?*

Solution: By pressing "sine 25," the value shown is 0.42261826... , which rounds off to 0.4226.

You recall that we defined the sine value as a ratio of the opposite side to the hypotenuse in a right triangle. The number 0.4226 could represent the ratio $\frac{4226}{10,000}$. This means that if the side opposite the angle θ were 4226 units and the hypotenuse were 10,000 units, θ would be about 25°. Of course, there are other ratios equivalent to $\frac{4226}{10,000}$, such as $\frac{2113}{5000}$.

Thus, if the side opposite angle θ were 2113 units and the hypotenuse were 5000, θ would still be about 25°.

2 **Example:**   **Consider the following right triangle.**

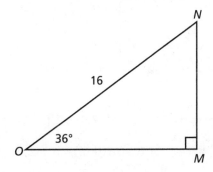

To the nearest hundredth, what is the value of MN?

Solution: Let y represent the value of *MN*. Then $\sin 36° = \frac{y}{16}$. Since $\sin 36° \approx 0.5878$, we have $0.5878 = \frac{y}{16}$. To solve this equation, we multiply both sides by 16. Since $(16)\left(\frac{y}{16}\right) = y$, we can write $y = (16)(0.5878) \approx 9.40$.

3 **Example:** *Consider the following right triangle.*

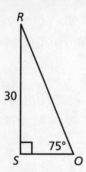

To the nearest hundredth, what is the value of RO?

Solution: Although the angle at point *O* is not in standard position, we could reposition it to appear as follows:

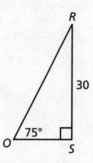

Let *r* represent the value of *RO,* which is the hypotenuse.

Then $\sin 75° = \dfrac{30}{r}$. Since $\sin 75° \approx 0.9659$, we have $0.9659 = \dfrac{30}{r}$.

Multiply both sides of this equation by *r* to get $0.9659r = 30$.

Then $r = \dfrac{30}{0.9659} \approx 31.06$.

4 **Example:** *Consider the following right triangle.*

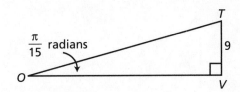

To the nearest hundredth, what is the value of OT?

Solution: Notice that the angle measure is given in radians, not degrees. Fortunately, you do not need to spend time in converting from radians to degrees. You can just reset your calculator to "radian" mode. Let r represent *OT*. Then $\sin \dfrac{\pi}{15}$ rad $= \dfrac{9}{r}$.

Since $\sin \dfrac{\pi}{15}$ rad ≈ 0.2079, we have $0.2079 = \dfrac{9}{r}$.
Multiply by r to get $0.2079r = 9$. Finally, $r \approx 43.29$.

MathFlash!

If you were insistent on only using degree measure for $\angle O$, you could first change $\dfrac{\pi}{15}$ radians to 12°. Since $\sin 12° \approx 0.2079$, you will get the same value for r.

5 **Example:**   *Consider the following triangle.*

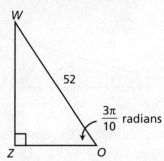

To the nearest hundredth, what is the value of WZ?

Solution: Let *y* represent *WZ*. Then $\sin \dfrac{3\pi}{10} = \dfrac{y}{52}$. Leaving your calculator in

"radian" mode, $\sin \dfrac{3\pi}{10} \approx 0.8090$. So, $0.8090 = \dfrac{y}{52}$. Multiply both

sides by 52 to get $y = (0.8090)(52) \approx 42.07$. Another way to solve

this example would be to change $\dfrac{3\pi}{10}$ radians to 54°.

1.   **Which one of the following is a quadrantal angle in standard position?**

(A)
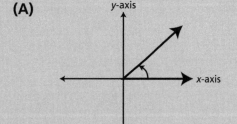

(C)
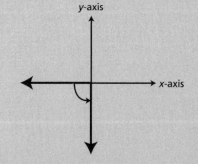

(B)
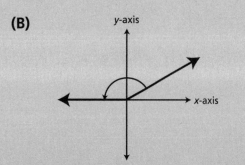

(D)
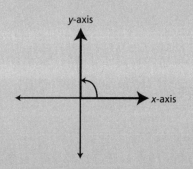

 **Test Yourself!** (continued)

2. Which feature determines that the measure of an angle is positive?

    (A) The angle is in standard position.

    (B) The angle is obtuse.

    (C) The direction of measurement is counterclockwise.

    (D) The direction of measurement is clockwise.

3. Look at the following triangle.

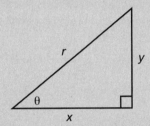

    Which one of the following represents sin θ?

    (A) $\dfrac{y}{r}$ (C) $\dfrac{r}{x}$

    (B) $\dfrac{x}{r}$ (D) $\dfrac{r}{y}$

4. To the nearest ten-thousandth, what is the value of sin 21°?

    Answer: _____

5. To the nearest ten-thousandth, what is the value of sin $\dfrac{4\pi}{9}$ rad?

    Answer: _____

 Test Yourself! *(continued)*

6.   Where does the initial ray of an obtuse angle lie when the angle is placed in standard position?

(A)   On the *y*-axis

(B)   In quadrant I

(C)   In quadrant II

(D)   On the *x*-axis

7.   Consider right △*OAC*, as shown below.

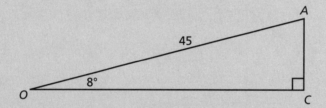

To the nearest hundredth, what is the value of *AC*?

Answer: _____

8.   Consider right △*OEG*, as shown below.

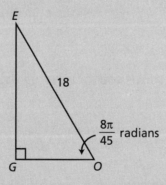

To the nearest hundredth, what is the value of *EG*?

Answer: _____

 **Test Yourself!** (continued)

9.   Consider right △*OHK*, as shown below.

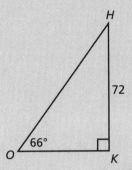

To the nearest hundredth, what is the value of *OH*?

Answer: _____

10.   Consider right △*OMR*, as shown below.

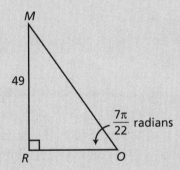

To the nearest hundredth, what is the value of *OM*?

Answer: _____

Basics of Trigonometric Ratios—Part 2

In this lesson, we will explore the method in which the **sine ratio** is calculated for angles in each of quadrants II, III, and IV. The **cosine ratio** will also be introduced and explained for all four quadrants.

Your Goal: When you have completed this lesson, you should be able to determine the sine ratio and cosine ratio for any angles between 0° and 360°. In addition, you will be able to determine the missing lengths of sides of a right triangle.

LESSON 3

Basics of Trigonometric Ratios—Part 2

Before we explore the values of the sine ratio in quadrants II, III, and IV, let's return to Figure 2.7 of Lesson 3, which has been drawn below, labeled as Figure 2.7a:

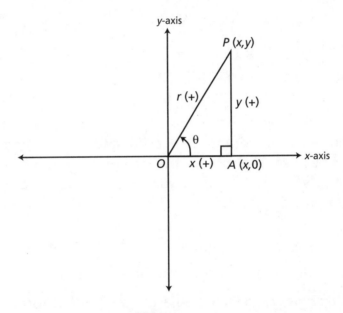

Figure 2.7a

Both of the numbers that represent the coordinates of point P are positive. This is expected, since θ is an angle in standard position that lies in the first quadrant. In Figure 2.7a, we have put + or – signs in parentheses attached to each of x, y, and r. The sine ratio, $\dfrac{y}{r}$, represents the quotient of two positive numbers. Thus, this ratio must be positive. The value of $\sin \theta$ was positive for each example and drill exercise of Lesson 2. As in Lesson 2, we are assuming that all angles are being measured in a counterclockwise direction.

Now consider θ as an angle in standard position that lies in the second quadrant, as shown in Figure 3.1.

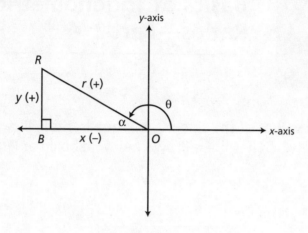

Figure 3.1

For right ΔOBR, notice that y and r have plus signs, but that x has a minus sign. Since point R is in the second quadrant, its x-coordinate must be negative and its y-coordinate must be positive. **The rule for the sign of r is that it is always positive.** Since the sine ratio involves only y and r, its value will still be the quotient of two positive numbers; thus, it will be positive.

You are surely concerned about the symbol α (pronounced "al' fuh") that appears inside ΔOBR at point O. By the definition of the sine ratio, $\sin \alpha = \dfrac{y}{r}$. This implies that sin α = sin θ. Since the angles α and θ are adjacent angles that form a straight line, their sum must be 180°.

Another way to state this information is as follows:
α = 180° − θ, **and so** sin θ = sin(180° − θ) **whenever θ is an obtuse angle.**
For example, if θ were 120°, 180° − θ = 60°.
Then sin 120° = sin 60°.
Using radian measure, sin θ = sin (π − θ), for any obtuse angle θ.

MathFlash!

Since θ and 180° − θ are really interchangeable, sin θ = sin(180° − θ) is true even if θ is an acute angle. For example, if θ = 35°, then 180° − θ = 145°, and we can state that sin 35° = sin 145°, whose value is about 0.4677.

As another example, using your calculator, you can determine that sin 68° = sin 112° ≈ 0.9272. Using radian measure, remember that 180° is equivalent to π radians. Thus, sin $\frac{\pi}{5}$ radians = sin $\frac{4\pi}{5}$ radians ≈ 0.5878.

Now consider θ as an angle in standard position that lies in the third quadrant, as shown below in Figure 3.2.

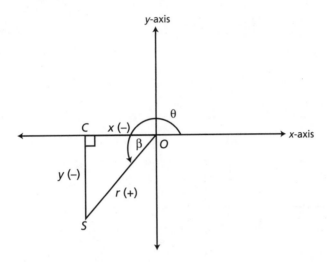

Figure 3.2

For right ΔOCS, both x and y have minus signs, but r still has a plus sign. Since point S is in the third quadrant, both its x-coordinate and y-coordinate must be negative. Now the sine ratio still involves y and r, but notice that the quotient of signs is a negative divided by a positive. Therefore, the value of sin θ must be negative.

What about the angle indicated by β (pronounce "bay' tuh") inside ΔOCS? We can easily see that β is an acute angle, and we know that the sine of an acute angle must be positive.

This implies that sin β is the <u>positive</u> value of the ratio $\frac{y}{r}$, whereas sin θ is the <u>negative</u> value of the ratio $\frac{y}{r}$. Let's determine how the measures of θ and β are related to each other. In Figure 3.2, the measure of θ minus the measure of β is 180°. Mathematically, θ – β = 180°, which can be expressed as β = θ – 180°.

Since sin θ and sin β differ by just a sign (+ or –), we can state that for any angle θ that lies in the third quadrant, sin θ = – sin (θ – 180). As an example, if θ = 225°, then θ – 180° = 45°. Using our calculator, we can check that sin 225° = – sin 45° ≈ –0.5736.

As an example with radian measure, let θ = $\frac{4\pi}{3}$. Then sin $\frac{4\pi}{3}$ = –sin $\frac{\pi}{3}$ ≈ –0.8660.

MathFlash!

$\sin \dfrac{4\pi}{3}$ means $\sin \dfrac{4\pi}{3}$ *radians. Whenever the degree symbol is omitted in referring to any trigonometric ratio, the measurement will* <u>*always*</u> *be assumed to be radians.*

Now consider θ as an angle in standard position that lies in the fourth quadrant, as shown in Figure 3.3.

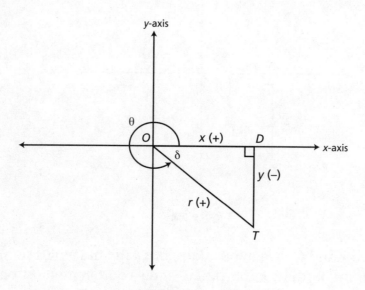

Figure 3.3

The value of θ must be between 270° and 360°. (In radian measure, θ must be between $\dfrac{3\pi}{2}$ radians and 2π radians). For right △*ODT*, both *x* and *r* have plus signs, but *y* has a minus sign. Since point *T* is in the fourth quadrant, its *x*-coordinate must be positive and its *y*-coordinate must be negative. The sine ratio still involves the ratio $\dfrac{y}{r}$. The quotient of signs is a negative divided by a positive, which results in a negative. Thus, sin θ must be a negative number whenever 270° < θ < 360°. Using radian measure, this inequality can be written as $\dfrac{3\pi}{2} < \theta < 2$. (Remember that when no units of measurement are shown, angles are assumed to be in radian measure.)

What about the angle indicated by δ (pronounced "dell' tuh") inside △*ODT*? Similar to the previous figures, we know that δ is an acute angle. This means that sin δ must be the positive value of the ratio $\dfrac{y}{r}$, even though sin θ is the corresponding negative value.

In studying Figure 3.3, we can see that $\theta + \delta = 360°$. This can also be written as $\delta = 360° - \theta$. Since $\sin \theta$ and $\sin \delta$ differ by just a sign (+ or –), we can state that for any angle θ that lies in the fourth quadrant, $\sin \theta = -\sin(360 - \theta)$. If radian measure is being used, simply replace $360°$ with 2π radians.

As an example, if $\theta = 330°$, then $360° - \theta = 30°$. Then $\sin 330° = -\sin 30° = -0.5000$.

As a second example, but using radian measure, if $\theta = \dfrac{17\pi}{10}$, then $2\pi - \theta = \dfrac{3\pi}{10}$.
Then $\sin \dfrac{17\pi}{10} = -\sin \dfrac{3\pi}{10} \approx -0.8090$.

Let's **summarize** our conclusions concerning the **value of sin θ for all four quadrants**. We'll use degree measurements for θ in each example, but these conclusions can be extended to radian measurements. As a reminder, $0° = 0$ radians, $90° = \dfrac{\pi}{2}$ radians, $180 = \pi$ radians, $270° = \dfrac{3\pi}{2}$ radians, and $360° = 2\pi$ radians.

In each case, θ is an angle in standard position.

   (A) If θ is in the first quadrant, then $\sin \theta$ is a positive number.

   (B) If θ is in the second quadrant, then $\sin \theta$ is a positive number.
        Also, $\sin \theta = \sin(180° - \theta)$.

   (C) If θ is in the third quadrant, then $\sin \theta$ is a negative number.
        Also, $\sin \theta = -\sin(\theta - 180°)$.

   (D) If θ is in the fourth quadrant, then $\sin \theta$ is a negative number.
        Also, $\sin \theta = -\sin(360 - \theta)$.

Of course, each of these statements can be written in radian form. Just substitute π for $180°$ and substitute 2π for $360°$.

At this point, we need to introduce the concept of a reference angle. If θ is an angle in standard position, then the **reference angle** of θ is the smallest positive angle between the terminal side of θ and the x-axis. Thus, the reference angle must be less than $90°$. In Figure 2.7a, the reference angle of θ is θ. Thus, when $0 < \theta < 90°$, there is no difference between θ and its reference angle.

In Figure 3.1, the reference angle of θ is α. Thus, when $90° < \theta < 180°$, the reference angle of θ is determined by evaluating $180° - \theta$.

In Figure 3.2, the reference angle of θ is β. Thus, when $180° < \theta < 270°$, the reference angle of θ is determined by evaluating $\theta - 180°$.

Finally, in Figure 3.3, the reference angle of θ is δ. Thus, when 270° < θ < 360°, the reference angle of θ is determined by evaluating 360° − θ.

Although we have only discussed the sine ratio, the rules for finding the reference angle apply for all trigonometric ratios. As you would expect, these rules also apply if θ is measured in radians.

We now introduce a second trigonometric ratio called **cosine**. Let's revisit Figure 2.7a:

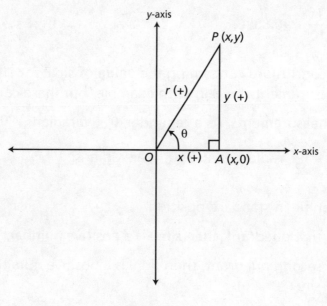

Figure 2.7a

Cosine θ, read as "the cosine of theta" is defined to be the ratio of the length of the adjacent side of this triangle (represented as *x*) to the length of the hypotenuse (represented as *r*). Cosine θ is commonly abbreviated as cos θ, so we can write

$$\cos θ = \frac{x}{r} = \frac{OA}{OP}.$$

Note that since *x* and *r* are positive, cos θ is positive for 0° < θ < 90°. We will now apply the definition of cosine to determining a missing side of a right triangle. Notice that your calculator has a button marked *cos*.

1 **Example:**   *To the nearest ten-thousandth, what is the value of cos 33°?*

Solution: By pressing *cos* followed by 33, the value shown is 0.8386705679…, which rounds off to 0.8387.

2 **Example:** *To the nearest ten-thousandth, what is the value of cos $\dfrac{2\pi}{7}$ rad?*

Solution: First be sure that your calculator is in "radian" mode. Then press cos followed by $\dfrac{2\pi}{7}$ to get the rounded off value of 0.6235.

3 **Example:** *Consider the following right triangle.*

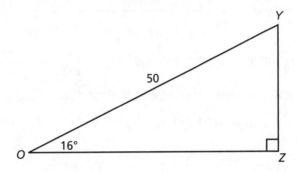

To the nearest hundredth, what is the value of OZ?

Solution: Let x represent the value of OZ. Then, by the definition of cosine, we get cos 16° = $\dfrac{x}{50}$. Since cos 16° ≈ 0.9613, x = (50)(0.9613) ≈ 48.07.

4 **Example:** *Consider the following right triangle.*

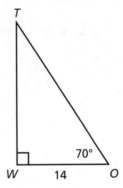

To the nearest hundredth, what is the value of OT?

Solution: Let r represent the value of OT. Then cos 70° = $\dfrac{14}{r}$. Using 0.3420 as the approximation for cos 70°, we have 0.3420 = $\dfrac{14}{r}$.

Multiply both sides of the equation by r to get 0.3420r = 14.

Finally, $r = \dfrac{14}{0.3420} ≈ 40.94$.

5 **Example:** *Consider the following right triangle.*

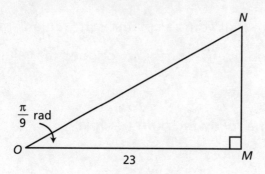

What is the value of ON?

Solution: Check to be sure your calculator is in "radian" mode. Let r represent the value of ON. Then $\cos \dfrac{\pi}{9} = \dfrac{23}{r}$. Since $\cos \dfrac{\pi}{9} \approx 0.9397$, we have $0.9397 = \dfrac{23}{r}$. Then $r = \dfrac{23}{0.9397} \approx 24.48$.

Now we will revisit Figure 3.1 in which θ lies in the second quadrant.

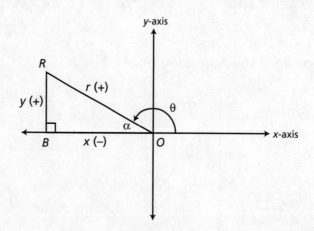

Figure 3.1

Since x is negative and r is positive, the ratio $\dfrac{x}{r}$ is negative. This implies that $\cos θ$ has a negative value when $90° < θ < 180°$. For right $\triangle OBR$, $\cos θ$ equals the negative value of the ratio $\dfrac{OB}{OR}$.

Just as with the sine ratio, the angle represented as α is related to θ for the cosine ratio. We already established that $\alpha = 180° - \theta$. Since α is an acute angle, $\cos \alpha$ must be the positive value of the ratio $\frac{x}{r}$. Thus, $\cos \theta = -\cos(180° - \theta)$, **whenever θ is an obtuse angle.** For example, suppose $\theta = 110°$. Then $\cos 110° = -\cos 70° \approx -0.3420$. As an example that uses radian measure, if $\theta = \frac{7\pi}{9}$ radians, then $\cos \frac{7\pi}{9} = -\cos \frac{2\pi}{9} \approx -0.7660$.

Now we will revisit Figure 3.2 in which θ lies in the third quadrant.

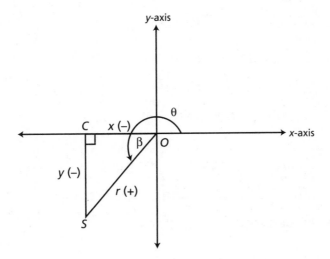

Figure 3.2

Since x is negative and r is positive, the ratio $\frac{x}{r}$ is negative. This implies that $\cos \theta$ has a negative value when $180° < \theta < 270°$. For right $\triangle OCS$, $\cos \theta$ equals the negative value of the ratio $\frac{OC}{OS}$.

As with the sine ratio, $\cos \beta$ is related to $\cos \theta$. We know that β is an acute angle, so that $\cos \beta$ is the positive value of $\frac{x}{r}$. In addition, we found out earlier in this lesson that $\beta = \theta - 180°$. Our conclusion must be that $\cos \theta = -\cos(\theta - 180°)$, **whenever θ lies in the third quadrant.** As an example, if $\theta = 260°$, then $\cos 260° = -\cos 80° \approx -0.1736$. As a different example with radian measure, if $\theta = \frac{10\pi}{9}$ radians, then $\cos \frac{10\pi}{9} = -\cos \frac{\pi}{9} \approx -0.9397$.

Finally, we will revisit Figure 3.3, shown below, in which θ lies in the fourth quadrant.

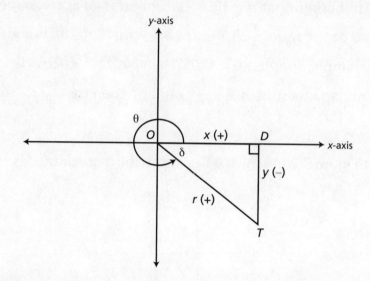

Figure 3.3

Since x is positive and r is positive, the ratio $\dfrac{x}{r}$ is positive. This implies that cos θ has a positive value when 270° < θ < 360°. For right $\triangle ODT$, $\cos\theta = \dfrac{x}{r} = \dfrac{OD}{OT}$. Let's now establish the relationship between cos θ and cos δ.

We already recall that δ is an acute angle, so that cos δ must equal the positive value of $\dfrac{x}{r}$.

Earlier in this lesson, we discovered that δ = 360° – θ.

Knowing that both cos θ and cos δ are equal to the positive value of $\dfrac{x}{r}$, we can conclude that cos θ = cos(360° – θ) **whenever θ lies in the fourth quadrant.**

As an example, suppose cos θ = 295°.
Then cos 295° = cos 65° ≈ 0.4226.

As a second example using radians, let $\theta = \dfrac{13\pi}{8}$ radians.

Since 360° is equivalent to 2π radians, 360° – θ becomes $2\pi - \dfrac{13\pi}{8} = \dfrac{3\pi}{8}$.

Then $\cos\dfrac{13\pi}{8} = \cos\dfrac{3\pi}{8} \approx 0.3827$.

Let's summarize our conclusions concerning the value of cos θ for all four quadrants. As before, we'll use degree measurements for θ in each example, but these conclusions can be extended to radian measurements:

(A) If θ is in the first quadrant, then cos θ is a positive number.

(B) If θ is in the second quadrant, then cos θ is a negative number. Also, cos θ = –cos(180° – θ).

(C) If θ is in the third quadrant, then cos θ is a negative number. Also, cos θ = –cos(θ – 180°).

(D) If θ is in the fourth quadrant, then cos θ is a positive number. Also, cos θ = cos(360° – θ).

Before you look at the next few examples, take a few minutes to review the conclusions concerning both sin θ and cos θ in all four quadrants.

6 Example: *Which one of the following is equivalent to sin 82°?*

    (A) sin 18°   *(C) sin 182°*

    (B) sin 98°   *(D) sin 278°*

Solution: The correct answer is (B). For any angle θ in the second quadrant, sin θ = sin(180° – θ). In this answer choice, θ = 82°.

7 Example: *Which one of the following is equivalent to sin $\dfrac{4\pi}{3}$ radians?*

    (A) sin $\dfrac{3\pi}{4}$ radians   *(C) sin $\dfrac{5\pi}{3}$ radians*

    (B) sin $\dfrac{\pi}{3}$ radians   *(D) sin $\dfrac{\pi}{4}$ radians*

Solution: The correct answer is (C). Since $\pi < \dfrac{4\pi}{3} < \dfrac{3\pi}{2}$, $\dfrac{4\pi}{3}$ radians lies in

the third quadrant. This means that sin $\dfrac{4\pi}{3} = -\sin \dfrac{\pi}{3}$, which is not

one of the answer choices. Answer choices (A) and (D) could not

possibly be right. Checking answer choice (C), since $\dfrac{3\pi}{2} < \dfrac{5\pi}{3} < 2\pi$,

$\dfrac{5\pi}{3}$ radians lies in the fourth quadrant. This means that

sin $\dfrac{5\pi}{3} = -\sin \dfrac{\pi}{3}$, which equals sin $\dfrac{4\pi}{3}$.

8   **Example:**   *Which one of the following is equivalent to cos 196°?*

(A) cos 164°   (C) cos 16°

(B) cos 96°   (D) cos 300°

Solution: The correct answer is (A). Since 196° lies in the third quadrant, cos 196° = −cos 16°. Now 164° lies in the second quadrant, so we have cos 164° = −cos 16°. Since both cos 196° and cos 164° equal −cos 16°, they must be equal to each other.

9   **Example:**   *Which one of the following is equivalent to $\cos \dfrac{\pi}{7}$ radians?*

(A) $\cos \dfrac{\pi}{14}$ radians   (C) $\cos \dfrac{8\pi}{7}$ radians

(B) $\cos \dfrac{3\pi}{5}$ radians   (D) $\cos \dfrac{13\pi}{7}$ radians

Solution: The correct answer is (D). Since $\dfrac{3\pi}{2} < \dfrac{13\pi}{7} < 2\pi$, $\dfrac{13\pi}{7}$ lies in the fourth quadrant. Then, $\cos \dfrac{13\pi}{7} = \cos\left(2\pi - \dfrac{13\pi}{7}\right) = \cos \dfrac{\pi}{7}$.

Answer choices (A) and (B) could not be right.

Note that answer choice (C) is wrong because $\cos \dfrac{8\pi}{7} = -\cos \dfrac{\pi}{7}$.

10   **Example:**   *If the measurement of an angle in standard position is $\dfrac{7\pi}{6}$ radians, what is the measure of its reference angle?*

Solution: Since $\pi < \dfrac{7\pi}{6} < \dfrac{3\pi}{2}$, we know that the angle in standard position lies in the third quadrant. Then the measure of the reference angle must be $\dfrac{7\pi}{6} - \pi = \dfrac{\pi}{6}$ radians.

1.   To the nearest ten-thousandth, what is the value of cos $\frac{5\pi}{13}$ rad?

Answer: _____

2.   Which one of the following has the same value as cos 150°

(A)   cos 30°   (C)   cos 210°

(B)   cos 120°   (D)   cos 300°

3.   If the measure of an angle in standard position is 342°, what is the measure of its reference angle?

Answer: _____

4.   Which one of the following has the same value as cos $\frac{12\pi}{7}$ radians?

(A)   cos $\frac{6\pi}{7}$ radians   (C)   cos $\frac{4\pi}{7}$ radians

(B)   cos $\frac{5\pi}{7}$ radians   (D)   cos $\frac{2\pi}{7}$ radians

5.   In a right triangle, the cosine of an angle means the ratio of the _____?

(A)   opposite side divided by the hypotenuse

(B)   adjacent side divided by the hypotenuse

(C)   hypotenuse divided by the opposite side

(D)   opposite side divided by the adjacent side

 *Test Yourself!* (continued)

6. The value of the cosine of an angle is positive in which quadrant(s)?

(A) Only in the first quadrant

(B) Only in the first and fourth quadrants

(C) Only in the third quadrant

(D) Only in the third and fourth quadrants

7. Consider the following right triangle.

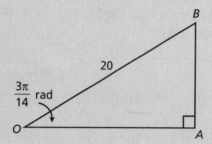

To the nearest hundredth, what is the value of *OA*?

Answer: _____

8. Consider the following right triangle.

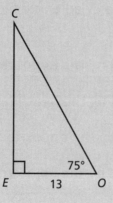

What is the value of *OC* to the nearest hundredth?

Answer: _____

 (continued)

9. **Consider the following right triangle.**

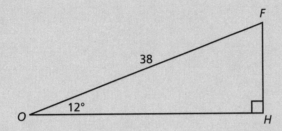

What is the value of *OH* to the nearest hundredth?

Answer: _____

10. **Consider the following right triangle.**

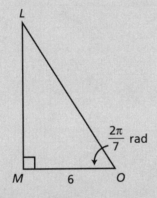

To the nearest hundredth, what is the value of *OL*?

Answer: _____

Basics of Trigonometric Ratios—Part 3

In this lesson, we will explore the method in which the **tangent ratio** is calculated for angles in each quadrant. Also, the relationships that exist among the **sine**, **cosine**, and **tangent ratios** will be explored.

Your Goal: When you have completed this lesson, you should be able to determine the tangent ratio for any angles between 0° and 360°. In addition, you will be able to determine the missing lengths of sides of a right triangle.

LESSON 4

Basics of Trigonometric Ratios—Part 3

We now introduce a third trigonometric ratio called **tangent**. In Figures 4.1 and 4.2, shown below, a right triangle is drawn in each of quadrants I and II, with the appropriate signs.

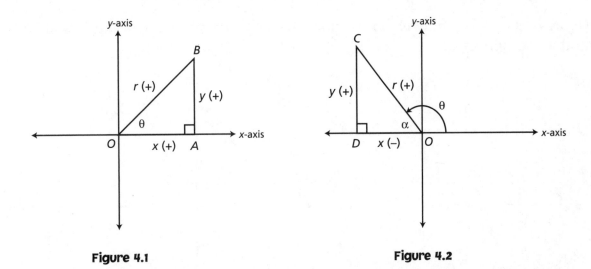

Figure 4.1   Figure 4.2

Tangent θ, (read as "the tangent of theta"), is defined to be the ratio of the length of the opposite side of the right triangle to the length of its adjacent side. **Tangent θ** is commonly abbreviated as tan θ. For $\triangle OAB$, we can write $\tan \theta = \dfrac{AB}{OA}$. Likewise, for $\triangle OCD$, $\tan \theta = \dfrac{CD}{OD}$.

Notice that tan θ must have a <u>positive</u> value when θ lies the first quadrant, as shown in Figure 4.1, since it represents a ratio of two positive values.

If θ lies in the second quadrant, as shown in Figure 4.2, then tan θ must have a <u>negative</u> value. This results from a ratio of a positive value (opposite side) divided by a negative value (adjacent side).

In terms of x, y, and r, we can state that $\tan\theta = \dfrac{y}{x}$ for all quadrants.

As we discovered about the sine ratio and cosine ratio for the second quadrant, $\alpha = 180° - \theta$. We know that since α is an acute angle, $\tan\alpha$ must be positive. Thus, $\tan\theta = -\tan(180° - \theta)$, **whenever θ lies in the second quadrant.** For example, suppose $\theta = 125°$. Your calculator provides a button marked *tan*, so you can verify that $\tan 125° = -\tan 55° \approx -1.4281$.

As an example using radian measure, let $\theta = \dfrac{4\pi}{5}$.

Then $\tan\dfrac{4\pi}{5} = -\tan\left(\pi - \dfrac{4\pi}{5}\right) = -\tan\dfrac{\pi}{5} \approx -0.7265$.

In Figures 4.3 and 4.4, shown below, a right triangle is drawn in quadrants III and IV, with the appropriate signs.

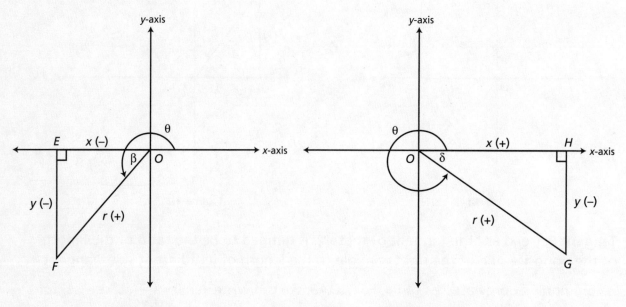

| Figure 4.3 | Figure 4.4 |

Notice that $\tan\theta$ must have a <u>positive</u> value when θ lies in the third quadrant, since it represents the ratio of two negative values. (Remember that a negative number divided by a negative number yields a positive number.) Since β is an acute angle, $\tan\beta$ must be positive. Since $\beta = \theta - 180°$, $\tan\theta = \tan(\theta - 180°)$ **whenever θ lies in the third quadrant.** As an example, suppose $\theta = 200°$. Then $\tan 200° = \tan 20° \approx 0.3640$.

Finally, if θ lies in the fourth quadrant, $\tan\theta$ is a ratio of a negative value divided by a positive value, which is a <u>negative</u> value. Since δ is an acute angle, $\tan\delta$ must be positive. Since $\delta = 360° - \theta$, $\tan\theta = -\tan(360° - \theta)$ **whenever θ lies in the fourth quadrant.** As an example, suppose $\theta = 285°$. Then $\tan 285° = -\tan(75°) \approx -3.7321$.

Summary of the value of tan θ for all four quadrants:

(Remember that these conclusions apply to both degree and radian measures.)

(a) If θ is in the first quadrant, then tan θ is a positive number.

(b) If θ is in the second quadrant, then tan θ is a negative number.
Also, tan θ = −tan(180° − θ).

(c) If θ is in the third quadrant, then tan θ is a positive number.
Also, tan θ = tan(θ − 180°) .

(d) If θ is in the fourth quadrant, then tan θ is a negative number.
Also, tan θ = −tan(360° − θ).

MathFlash!

*An easy way to remember in which quadrants each of the three trigonometric ratios are positive is to think of the phrase "Save All The Children." As a diagram, these letters appear as shown in Figure 4.5, where **S** = sine, **A** = all, **T** = tangent, and **C** = cosine.*

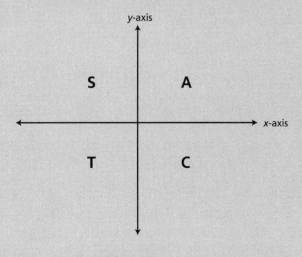

Figure 4.5

*In this way, you immediately know that in the **third quadrant**, the tangent ratio is <u>positive</u>, but both the sine ratio and cosine ratio are <u>negative</u>.*

Let's try a few examples in which **angle relationships** are used. Also, we can apply the tangent ratio to finding a missing side of a right triangle.

1 **Example:** *Which one of the following is equivalent to tan 78°?*

(A) tan 12°　　　　　　　　(C) tan 168°

(B) tan 282°　　　　　　　 (D) tan 258°

Solution: The correct answer is (D). For any angle in the third quadrant, $\tan\theta = \tan(\theta - 180°)$, which must be positive. Here, $\theta = 258°$. To check: $258° - 180° = 78°$.

2 **Example:** *Which one of the following is equivalent to* $\tan\dfrac{9\pi}{5}$ *rad?*

(A) $\tan\dfrac{5\pi}{9}$ rad　　　　　　(C) $\tan\dfrac{\pi}{5}$ rad

(B) $\tan\dfrac{4\pi}{5}$ rad　　　　　　(D) $\tan\dfrac{4\pi}{9}$ rad

Solution: The correct answer is (B). Since $\dfrac{3\pi}{2} < \dfrac{9\pi}{5} < 2\pi$, we know that

$\dfrac{9\pi}{5}$ rad lies in the fourth quadrant. This means that $\tan\dfrac{9\pi}{5}$ rad must have a negative value. Its value is equivalent to

$$-\tan\left(2\pi - \frac{9\pi}{5}\right) = -\tan\frac{\pi}{5} \text{ rad}.$$

The only other quadrant where the tangent ratio is negative

is the second quadrant. Since $\dfrac{\pi}{2} < \dfrac{4\pi}{5} < \pi$, we know that

$\dfrac{4\pi}{5}$ lies in the second quadrant. Its value is equivalent to

$$-\tan\left(\pi - \frac{4\pi}{5}\right) = -\tan\frac{\pi}{5}.$$

As a final check, $\tan\dfrac{9\pi}{5}$ rad $= \tan\dfrac{5\pi}{9}$ rad ≈ -0.7265.

3 **Example:**   *Consider the following right triangle.*

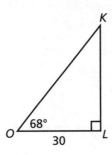

What is the value of KL to the nearest hundredth?

Solution: Let y represent the value of *KL*. Then $\tan 68° = \dfrac{y}{30}$.

Since $\tan 68° \approx 2.4751$, $y = (30)(2.4751) \approx 74.25$.

4 **Example:**   *Consider the following right triangle.*

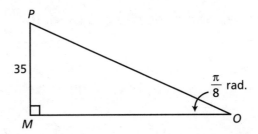

What is the value of OM to the nearest hundredth?

Solution: Let x represent the value of *OM*. Then $\tan \dfrac{\pi}{8}$ rad $= \dfrac{35}{x}$.

Using 0.4142 as the approximate value of $\tan \dfrac{\pi}{8}$, we get $0.4142 = \dfrac{35}{x}$.

This becomes $0.4142x = 35$, so $x = \dfrac{35}{0.4142} \approx 84.50$.

Now let's consider **the relationship among the sine, cosine, and tangent ratios**. Look at the right triangle, shown below in Figure 4.6.

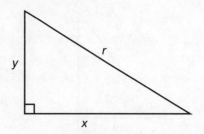

Figure 4.6

We have learned that $\sin\theta = \dfrac{y}{r}$, $\cos\theta = \dfrac{x}{r}$, and $\tan\theta = \dfrac{y}{x}$. There is a definite relationship among these three ratios. Notice that $\dfrac{y}{r} \div \dfrac{x}{r} = \dfrac{y}{r} \times \dfrac{r}{x} = \dfrac{y}{x}$.

This means that $\dfrac{\sin\theta}{\cos\theta} = \tan\theta$.

- This certainly is correct when θ lies in quadrant I, in which all ratios are positive. Due to the fact that the signs change (+, –) when looking at these ratios in the other quadrants, we need to check if $\dfrac{\sin\theta}{\cos\theta} = \tan\theta$ is true, regardless of the value of θ.

- In quadrant II, $\sin\theta$ is positive, $\cos\theta$ is negative, and $\tan\theta$ is negative. Since a positive number divided by a negative number yields a negative number, this is *OK*.

- In quadrant III, $\sin\theta$ is negative, $\cos\theta$ is negative, and $\tan\theta$ is positive. Since a negative number divided by a negative number yields a positive number, this is *OK*.

- In quadrant IV, $\sin\theta$ is negative, $\cos\theta$ is positive, and $\tan\theta$ is negative. Since a negative number divided by a positive number yields a negative number, this is *OK*.

Let's check $\dfrac{\sin\theta}{\cos\theta} = \tan\theta$ by using values of θ in different quadrants.

If $\theta = 123°$, then $\sin\theta \approx 0.8387$, $\cos\theta \approx -0.5446$, and $\tan\theta \approx -1.5399$.

Sure enough, $-1.5399 \approx \dfrac{0.8387}{-0.5446}$. (The error is about 0.0001, due to rounding.)

If $\theta = \dfrac{5\pi}{3}$ radians, then $\sin\theta \approx -0.8660$, $\cos\theta = 0.5000$, and $\tan\theta \approx -1.7321$.

Happily, we find that $-1.7321 \approx \dfrac{-0.8660}{0.5000}$. (Again, just a slight error due to rounding.)

Do you recall the **Pythagorean theorem**? This theorem says that given a right triangle, **the sum of the squares of the two shorter sides is equal to the square of the hypotenuse.** Applying this theorem to Figure 4.6, we can write $x^2 + y^2 = r^2$. In fact, even if θ is found in any of the other quadrants, $x^2 + y^2 = r^2$ is still correct. Notice that each of x^2, y^2, and r^2 is positive, even if either of x or y is negative.

You may be wondering if this information is important. It is!
Let's write the expression $(\sin \theta)^2 + (\cos \theta)^2$ in terms of x, y, and r.

By substitution, $(\sin \theta)^2 + (\cos \theta)^2 = \left(\dfrac{y}{r}\right)^2 + \left(\dfrac{x}{r}\right)^2 = \dfrac{y^2}{r^2} + \dfrac{x^2}{r^2} = \dfrac{y^2 + x^2}{r^2} = \dfrac{r^2}{r^2} = 1$.

This means that **for any angle θ, the sum of the squares of the sine and cosine of that angle must be 1.**

MathFlash!

The square of a trigonometric ratio such as $(\sin \theta)^2$ is commonly written as $\sin^2 \theta$. Likewise, $(\cos \theta)^2$ may be written as $\cos^2 \theta$, and $(\tan \theta)^2$ may be written a $\tan^2 \theta$. CAUTION: Be sure you do <u>not</u> square the angle θ!

5 **Example:**   *If $\sin \theta = 0.6561$ and $\cos \theta = 0.7547$, then to the nearest ten-thousandth, what is the value of $\tan \theta$?*

Solution: $\dfrac{\sin \theta}{\cos \theta} = \tan \theta$, so by substitution, $\dfrac{0.6561}{0.7547} \approx 0.8694$.
(Incidentally, since all three trigonometric ratios are positive, θ lies in the first quadrant.)

We can use the numbers in Example 5 to verify that $\sin^2 \theta + \cos^2 \theta = 1$. By substitution, $(0.6561)^2 + (0.7547)^2 \approx 0.4305 + 0.5696 = 1.0001$. The error is only 0.0001 and is due strictly to rounding.

6 Example: *If tan θ = 0.3541 and sin θ = –0.3338, then what is the value of cos θ to the nearest ten-thousandth?*

Solution: Since the tangent ratio is positive and the sine ratio is negative, θ must lie in the third quadrant. This means that the cosine ratio is negative.

Substituting into $\dfrac{\sin \theta}{\cos \theta} = \tan \theta$, we get $\dfrac{-0.3338}{\cos \theta} \approx 0.3541$.

Multiply both sides of the equation by cos θ to get $-0.3338 = 0.3541 \cos \theta$.

Then $\cos \theta = \dfrac{-0.3338}{0.3541} \approx -0.9427$.

7 Example: *If $\cos \theta = \dfrac{2}{3}$ and θ lies in the fourth quadrant, then what is the value of sin θ to the nearest ten-thousandth?*

Solution: Using the formula $\sin^2 \theta + \cos^2 \theta = 1$, and substituting the value of cos θ, we get $\sin^2 \theta + \left(\dfrac{2}{3}\right)^2 = 1$. Simplify this equation to $\sin^2 \theta + \dfrac{4}{9} = 1$, which becomes $\sin^2 \theta = \dfrac{5}{9}$. Then $\sin \theta = \sqrt{\dfrac{5}{9}} \approx 0.7454$.

This is <u>not</u> the final answer!

Since θ lies in the fourth quadrant, sin θ <u>must</u> be negative.

Thus, the final answer is –0.7454.

8 **Example:**   *If $\tan \theta = -\dfrac{5}{2}$ and θ lies in the second quadrant, what is the value of cos θ to the nearest ten-thousandth?*

Solution: At first glance, this question may seem like "Mission Impossible," since we are not given the value of sin θ. Since the definition of tan θ is the ratio of the opposite side to the adjacent side in a right triangle, we can sketch the problem as shown below.

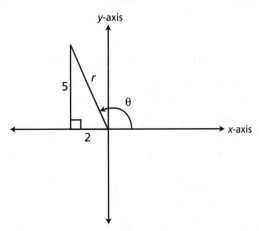

In order to determine the value of cos θ, we must know the value of *r*. The good news is that we can use the Pythagorean theorem, so that $2^2 + 5^2 = r^2$. This equation simplifies to $4 + 25 = 29 = r^2$, so $r = \sqrt{29} \approx 5.3852$. Since cos θ is the ratio of the adjacent side to the hypotenuse, we calculate $\dfrac{2}{5.3852} \approx 0.3714$.

Since θ lies in the second quadrant, our final answer is –0.3714.

9 **Example:**   *Refer back to the information given in Example 8. What is the value of sin θ to the nearest ten-thousandth?*

Solution: There are really two solid ways to find sin θ. One way is to use the formula $\sin^2 \theta + \cos^2 \theta = 1$. From Example 8, we determined that cos θ ≈ –0.3714. By substitution, $\sin^2 \theta + (-0.3714)^2 = 1$.

This equation simplifies to $\sin^2 \theta = 1 - (-0.3714)^2 \approx 1 - 0.1379 = 0.8621$. Then $\sin \theta = \sqrt{0.8621} \approx 0.9285$.

The answer must be positive because the sine ratio is positive in the second quadrant.

MathFlash!

Can you see another way to find the solution to Example 9? We could have used the equation $\frac{\sin\theta}{\cos\theta} = \tan\theta$. Then $\frac{\sin\theta}{-0.3714} = -2.5$. (We changed $-\frac{5}{2}$ to –2.5.) Now multiply both sides by –0.3714 to get $\sin\theta = (-2.5)(-0.3714) = 0.9285$.

10   Example: *If $\sin\theta = 0.65$ and θ lies in the first quadrant, then what are the values of $\cos\theta$ and $\tan\theta$ to the nearest ten-thousandth?*

Solution: The quickest way to find the value of $\cos\theta$ is to use the formula $\sin^2\theta + \cos^2\theta = 1$. By substitution, $(0.65)^2 + \cos^2\theta = 1$. Then $\cos^2\theta = 1 - 0.4225 = 0.5775$. So $\cos\theta = \sqrt{0.5775} \approx 0.7599$.

Now using $\frac{\sin\theta}{\cos\theta} = \tan\theta$, we get $\tan\theta = \frac{0.65}{0.7599} \approx 0.8554$.

(Note that all three ratios are positive, as you would expect when θ lies in the first quadrant.)

Test Yourself!

1.   If $\tan\theta$ has a positive value, then in which quadrant(s) does θ lie?

   (A)   Only in quadrants I and IV

   (B)   Only in quadrant I

   (C)   Only in quadrants I and III

   (D)   Only in quadrant III

2.   If θ is measured in radians and lies in the fourth quadrant , then which one of the following is equivalent to $\tan\theta$?

   (A) $\tan(2\pi - \theta)$ (C) $-\tan(\theta - \pi)$

   (B) $-\tan(2\pi - \theta)$ (D) $\tan\left(\theta + \dfrac{\pi}{2}\right)$

 **Test Yourself!** (continued)

3. Which one of the following has the same value as tan 162°?

   (A) tan 342°   (C) tan 198°

   (B) tan 288°   (D) tan 62°

4. Consider the following right triangle.

   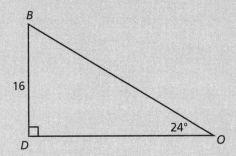

   What is the value of *OD* to the nearest hundredth?

                                          Answer: _____

5. Consider the following right triangle.

   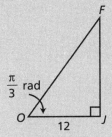

   What is the value of *FJ* to the nearest hundredth?

                                          Answer: _____

6. If sin θ = –0.4695 and cos θ = –0.8830, then what is the value of tan θ to the nearest ten-thousandth?

                                          Answer: _____

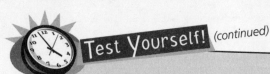

7. If $\cos \theta = \dfrac{3}{7}$ and θ lies in the fourth quadrant, then what is the value of $\sin \theta$ to the nearest ten-thousandth?

   (A)   0.8163

   (B)   0.9035

   (C)   −0.8163

   (D)   −0.9035

8. If $\tan \theta = \dfrac{8}{5}$ and θ lies in the third quadrant, then what is the value of $\sin \theta$ to the nearest ten-thousandth?

   (A)   0.8480

   (B)   0.5300

   (C)   −0.5300

   (D)   −0.8480

9. Which one of the following situations is <u>not</u> possible?

   (A) $\sin \theta = \dfrac{4}{5}$ and $\cos \theta = -\dfrac{3}{5}$

   (B) $\sin \theta = -\dfrac{2}{5}$ and $\cos \theta = -\dfrac{4}{5}$

   (C) $\sin \theta = \dfrac{5}{13}$ and $\cos \theta = \dfrac{12}{13}$

   (D) $\sin \theta = -\dfrac{8}{17}$ and $\cos \theta = -\dfrac{15}{17}$

10. Which one of the following situations is <u>not</u> possible?

   (A)   Each of $\sin \theta$, $\cos \theta$, and $\tan \theta$ is positive for a given θ.

   (B)   Sin θ is positive, but $\cos \theta$ and $\tan \theta$ are both negative for a given θ.

   (C)   Each of $\sin \theta$, $\cos \theta$, and $\tan \theta$ is negative for a given θ.

   (D)   Sin θ and $\cos \theta$ are negative, but $\tan \theta$ is positive for a given θ.

Basics of Trigonometric Ratios—Part 4

In this lesson, we will explore the remaining three trigonometric ratios, namely the **cosecant**, **secant**, and **cotangent**. Also, the key relationships that exist among all six trigonometric ratios will be explored.

Your Goal: When you have completed this lesson, you should be able to determine each of the trigonometric ratios for any angles between 0° and 360°. In addition, you will understand the connection among these ratios.

LESSON 5

Basics of Trigonometric Ratios—Part 4

Let's return to Figure 4.1, as shown below.

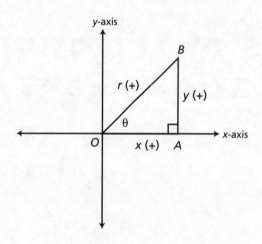

Figure 4.1

Cosecant θ is defined to be the ratio of the hypotenuse of a right triangle to the length of the opposite side. Cosecant θ is commonly abbreviated as csc θ, and is called the **reciprocal** ratio for sin θ.

In Figure 4.1, we can write $\csc \theta = \dfrac{OB}{AB}$.

Using the letters *x, y,* and *r* for any of the quadrants, $\csc \theta = \dfrac{r}{y}$.

Similar to the sine, cosine, and tangent ratios, the cosecant ratio may have a negative value. In fact, since its value is the reciprocal of the sine ratio, for a given value of θ, sin θ and csc θ must be either both positive or both negative.

We know that sin θ is positive in quadrants I and II, while negative in quadrants III and IV. This means that csc θ must also be positive in quadrants I and II, while negative in quadrants III and IV.

Thus, $\csc \theta = \dfrac{1}{\sin \theta}$, which is equivalent to (csc θ)(sin θ) = 1, is true regardless of the quadrant in which θ lies.

MathFlash!

In order to **calculate the value of csc θ**, you need to use the "sine" button on your calculator, as we will show in Example 1.

1 **Example:**   *What is the value of csc 40° to the nearest ten-thousandth?*

Solution: By definition, $\csc 40° = \dfrac{1}{\sin 40°}$. Just press the buttons *1* and *÷* followed by the buttons *sin* and *40*.

Be sure that your calculator is in "degree" mode.
The answer is 1.5557.

2 **Example:**   *To the nearest ten-thousandth, what is the value of* $\csc \dfrac{5\pi}{4}$ *radians?*

Solution: First, change the calculator mode to "radians." We need to calculate $\dfrac{1}{\sin \frac{5\pi}{4}}$. The answer is −1.4142.

Just press the buttons *1* and *÷* followed by the buttons *sin* and $\dfrac{5\pi}{4}$.
The answer is −1.4142.

Secant θ is defined as the ratio of the hypotenuse of a right triangle to the length of the adjacent side. Secant θ is commonly abbreviated as sec θ and is called the reciprocal ratio for cos θ.

In Figure 4.1, we can write $\sec \theta = \dfrac{OB}{OA}$. Using the letters *x*, *y*, and *r* for any of the quadrants, $\sec \theta = \dfrac{r}{x}$.

Can you guess in which quadrants the secant ratio is positive? You already know that the cosine ratio is positive in quadrants I and IV, while negative in quadrants II and III. Hopefully, you instantly realized that the same situation holds for the secant ratio. That is, sec θ is <u>positive</u> in quadrants I and IV, while <u>negative</u> in quadrants II and III.

Mathematically, $\sec\theta = \dfrac{1}{\cos\theta}$, which can also be written as $(\sec\theta)(\cos\theta) = 1$. This equation is true regardless of the quadrant in which θ lies.

Since the secant ratio is the reciprocal of the cosine ratio, we can find the value of sec θ by dividing 1 by cos θ.

3   **Example:**   *What is the value of* $\sec\dfrac{2\pi}{5}$ *radians to the nearest ten-thousandth?*

       Solution: $\sec\dfrac{2\pi}{5} = \dfrac{1}{\cos\dfrac{2\pi}{5}}$, so the answer is 3.2361.

MathFlash!

If you round off $\cos\dfrac{2\pi}{5}$ *to the nearest ten-thousandth first,*

$\cos\dfrac{2\pi}{5} \approx 0.3090$, *and then take its reciprocal,* $\dfrac{1}{0.3090} \approx 3.2362$, *your answer will only differ by one ten-thousandth. Your answer will still be very accurate.*

4   **Example:**   *What is the value of sec 303° to the nearest ten-thousandth?*

       Solution: $\sec 303° = \dfrac{1}{\cos 303°} \approx 1.8361$

Cotangent θ is defined as the ratio of the length of the adjacent side of a right triangle to the length of the opposite side. Cotangent θ is commonly abbreviated as cot θ and is called the reciprocal ratio for tan θ. This means that $\cot\theta = \dfrac{1}{\tan\theta}$, which can be written as (cot θ)(tan θ) = 1.

For Figure 4.1, we can write $\cot\theta = \dfrac{OA}{AB}$.

Using x, y, and r, for any of the quadrants, $\cot\theta = \dfrac{x}{y}$.

As with any of the other five trigonometric ratios, the sign of $\dfrac{x}{y}$ will be plus or minus, depending on the quadrant in which θ lies.

Since tan θ is positive in quadrants I and III, cot θ is also positive in quadrants I and III. It follows that both tan θ and cot θ are negative in quadrants II and IV.

5 **Example:**   *What is the value of cot 75° to the nearest ten-thousandth?*

Solution: We just need to divide 1 by tan 75°. Use the *tan* button on your calculator. The answer is $\dfrac{1}{\tan 75°} \approx 0.2679$.

6 **Example:**   *What is the value of* $\cot\dfrac{8\pi}{5}$ *radians to the nearest ten-thousandth?*

Solution: $\cot\dfrac{8\pi}{5} = \dfrac{1}{\tan\dfrac{8\pi}{5}} \approx -0.3249$

We have established two interesting trigonometric equations involving sin θ, cos θ, and tan θ. These equations were $\tan\theta = \dfrac{\sin\theta}{\cos\theta}$ and $\sin^2\theta + \cos^2\theta = 1$.

Since these equations are true for any value of θ, they are also called **trigonometric identities**.

A third trigonometric identity can be found by recognizing that $\cot\theta = \dfrac{1}{\tan\theta}$.

This means that $\cot\theta = \dfrac{1}{\dfrac{\sin\theta}{\cos\theta}} = \dfrac{\cos\theta}{\sin\theta}$.

A <u>fourth</u> trigonometric identity can be found as follows.

In our famous first quadrant right triangle:

a) x represents the adjacent side

b) y represents the opposite side, and

c) r represents the hypotenuse

d) Also, we know that $x^2 + y^2 = r^2$. Then $\tan^2 \theta + 1 = \dfrac{y^2}{x^2} + 1 = \dfrac{y^2}{x^2} + \dfrac{x^2}{x^2} = \dfrac{r^2}{x^2} = \sec^2 \theta$.

A <u>fifth</u> trigonometric identity can be found by using the equation $\cot \theta = \dfrac{x}{y}$.

Then, $\cot^2 \theta + 1 = \dfrac{x^2}{y^2} + 1 = \dfrac{x^2}{y^2} + \dfrac{y^2}{y^2} = \dfrac{r^2}{y^2} = \csc^2 \theta$.

7 **Example:**   *If $\cos \theta = \dfrac{2}{7}$, what is the value of sec θ?*

Solution: $\sec \theta = \dfrac{1}{\cos \theta} = \dfrac{1}{\frac{2}{7}} = \dfrac{7}{2}$.

MathFlash!

Note that we need not know if θ is in the first or fourth quadrant. Also, this answer is not affected by whether θ is measured in degrees or in radians.

8 **Example:**   *If csc θ = –2.1236, then to the nearest ten-thousandth, what is the value of sin θ?*

Solution: Since $(\csc \theta)(\sin \theta) = 1$, $\sin \theta = \dfrac{1}{\csc \theta} = \dfrac{1}{-2.1236} \approx -0.4709$.
Note that θ lies in either quadrant III or quadrant IV.

9 **Example:** *If tan θ = 0.2665, then to the nearest ten-thousandth, what is the value of sec θ?*

Solution: We need to use the formula $\tan^2 \theta + 1 = \sec^2 \theta$.
By substitution, we get $(0.2665)^2 + 1 = \sec^2 \theta$.
Then $\sec^2 \theta \approx 0.0710 + 1 = 1.0710$.
This means that $\sin \theta = \pm \sqrt{1.0710}$.
Then $\sec \theta \approx 1.0349$ or -1.0349.

MathFlash!

Example 9 has <u>two</u> answers, and for a very good reason! If tan θ is positive, then θ must lie in quadrant I or III. If θ lies in quadrant I, then sec θ must also be positive. But if θ lies in quadrant III, then sec θ must be negative.

10 **Example:** *If $\csc \theta = \dfrac{7}{6}$ and θ lies in the second quadrant, then what is the value of cot θ to the nearest ten-thousandth?*

Solution: We need to use the formula $\cot^2 \theta + 1 = \csc^2 \theta$.

By substitution, we get $\cot^2 \theta + 1 = \left(\dfrac{7}{6}\right)^2$.

Then $\cot^2 \theta = \left(\dfrac{7}{6}\right)^2 - 1 = \dfrac{49}{36} - 1 \approx 0.3611$.

Following the method we used in Example 9, our answers would normally be $\cot \theta = \pm\sqrt{0.3611} \approx 0.6009$ or -0.6009.
However, since θ lies in the second quadrant (in which cot θ must be negative), the <u>only</u> answer is −0.6009.

11 **Example:** *If* $\cot \theta = -\dfrac{7}{24}$ *and θ lies in the fourth quadrant, then what fraction represents the value of sin θ?*

Solution: Since we do not have a formula that contains both cot θ and sin θ, the easiest way to solve this problem is to use an appropriate diagram.

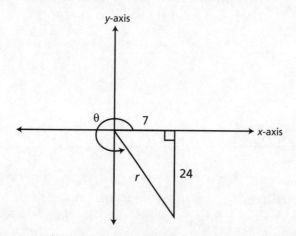

Using the Pythagorean theorem, $r^2 = 7^2 + 24^2 = 49 + 576 = 625$.

Then $r = \sqrt{625} = 25$. (Remember, r __must__ be positive.)

Now, by the definition of the sine ratio, $\sin \theta = -\dfrac{24}{25}$.

12 **Example:** *If* $\sin \theta = \dfrac{7}{10}$, *to the nearest ten-thousandth, what is the value of sec θ?*

Solution: Since we do not have a formula that contains both sin θ and sec θ, we'll again use an appropriate diagram. Be aware that the sine ratio is positive in __both__ the first and second quadrants. Let's use a diagram in quadrant I, as shown below.

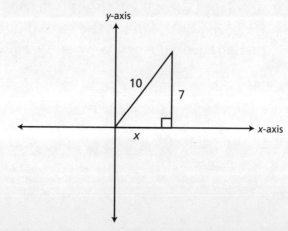

Using the Pythagorean theorem, $x^2 + 7^2 = 10^2$.
This equation becomes $x^2 = 10^2 - 7^2 = 100 - 49 = 51$.
Then $x = \sqrt{51} \approx 7.1414$.

Thus, using the definition of the secant ratio, $\sec \theta = \dfrac{10}{7.1414} \approx 1.4003$.

Don't stop here! If θ lies in quadrant II, then $\sec \theta$ must be negative. This means that the second answer is -1.4003.

Test Yourself!

1. If $\sin \theta = -\dfrac{9}{10}$, then what is the value of $\csc \theta$?

   Answer: _____

2. If $\sec \theta = -2.3362$, then what are the <u>two</u> values of $\tan \theta$ to the nearest ten-thousandth?

   Answer: _____

3. To the nearest ten-thousandth, what is the value of $\cot \dfrac{6\pi}{7}$ radians?

   Answer: _____

4. If $\csc \theta = 1.24$ and θ lies in the first quadrant, then what is the value of $\cot \theta$ to the nearest ten-thousandth?

   Answer: _____

5. In which quadrant would $\tan \theta$ have a negative value while $\csc \theta$ has a positive value?

   Answer: _____

6.   Which one of the following sets of conditions is not possible?

(A)   Tan θ has a positive value, and cos θ has a negative value.

(B)   Both sec θ and sin θ have negative values.

(C)   Both csc θ and cot θ have positive values.

(D)   Sin θ has a negative value, and csc θ has a positive value.

7.   If $\sec \theta = -\dfrac{17}{8}$ and θ lies in the second quadrant, then what fraction represents the value of sin θ?

Answer: _____

8.   If sin θ ≈ 0.56 and cos θ ≈ –0.83, then what is the value of cot θ to the nearest ten-thousandth?

Answer: _____

9.   If cot θ = 0.2345, then what are the two values of csc θ to the nearest ten-thousandth?

Answers: _____

10.   Which one of the following has the largest value?

(A) $\tan \dfrac{3\pi}{5}$ radians

(C)   sin 100°

(B) $\cot \dfrac{8\pi}{7}$ radians

(D)   sec 305°

QUIZ ONE

1. If $\cos \theta = -\dfrac{3}{5}$ and θ lies in the second quadrant, what is the value of $\sin \theta$?

   A $-\dfrac{4}{5}$ C $\dfrac{3}{4}$

   B $-\dfrac{3}{4}$ D $\dfrac{4}{5}$

2. If θ lies in the fourth quadrant, then which one of the following has the same value as $\tan \theta$?

   A $-\tan(\theta - 360°)$

   B $-\tan(360° - \theta)$

   C $-\tan(\theta - 90°)$

   D $-\tan(90° - \theta)$

3. How many radians are there in a right angle?

   A $\dfrac{\pi}{2}$ C $\dfrac{\pi}{90}$

   B $\dfrac{\pi}{4}$ D $\dfrac{\pi}{180}$

4. In which one of the following situations does the minute hand of a clock rotate through 150°?

   A Moving from the number 2 to the number 6

   B Moving from the number 3 to the number 11

   C Moving from the number 4 to the number 9

   D Moving from the number 5 to the number 12

5. Which one of the following describes the measurement of a positive angle in standard position?

   A Its initial ray is on the y-axis and it is measured in a clockwise direction.

   B Its initial ray is on the x-axis and it is measured in a counterclockwise direction.

   C Its initial ray is on the y-axis and it is measured in a counterclockwise direction.

   D Its initial ray is on the x-axis and it is measured in a clockwise direction.

6. If $\cot \theta \approx -2.5$ and $\sin \theta \approx 0.37$, what is the best approximation for the value of $\cos \theta$?

   A -0.15 C -0.93

   B -0.35 D -2.13

7. If $180° < \theta < 270°$, then the reference angle for θ is represented by which one of the following?

   A $\theta - 360°$ C $180° - \theta$

   B $360° - \theta$ D $\theta - 180°$

8. Consider right triangle *RON*, as shown below:

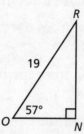

What is the value of *RN* to the nearest hundredth?

A 10.83   C 14.23

B 12.53   D 15.93

9. In which one of the following does θ have only one value?

A sin θ = –1   C tan θ = –2

B sec θ = 3   D csc θ = 4

10. Consider right triangle *AOD*, as shown below:

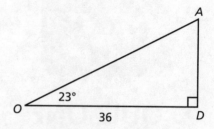

What is the value of *OA* to the nearest hundredth?

A 37.21   C 41.01

B 39.11   D 42.91

Special Angles and Trigonometric Ratio Values

In this lesson, we will explore the trigonometric ratios associated with **quadrantal angles** and with **angles related to special triangles**. We will also show how to locate more than one angle whose specific trigonometric ratio is the same.

Your Goal: When you have completed this lesson, you should be able to immediately calculate the value of certain trigonometric ratios.

LESSON 6

Special Angles and Trigonometric Ratio Values

As a review, a **quadrantal angle** is one whose initial ray lies on the *x*-axis and whose terminal ray coincides with the *x*-axis or *y*-axis. The four quadrantal angles to be discussed are 0°, 90°, 180°, and 270°. (We treat 360° the same as 0°.)

Consider Figure 6.1, which represents an angle of 0°. **In reality, there would be no $\triangle OAB$, because $\overline{OA}$ would lie on top of $\overline{OB}$.**

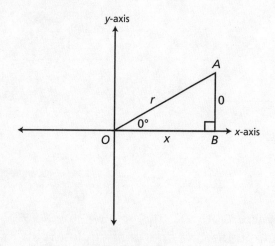

Figure 6.1

First notice that *y* has been replaced by *0*. Using the Pythagorean theorem, $x^2 + 0^2 = r^2$. Since *x* and *r* are both positive, this means that $x = r$.

Here are the values of the six trigonometric ratios when $\theta = 0°$:

$$\sin 0° = \frac{0}{r} = 0$$

$$\cos 0° = \frac{x}{r} = \frac{r}{r} = 1$$

$$\tan 0° = \frac{0}{x} = 0$$

$$\csc 0° = \frac{1}{\sin 0°} = \frac{1}{0} = \text{not defined}$$

$$\sec 0° = \frac{1}{\cos 0°} = \frac{1}{1} = 1$$

$$\cot 0° = \frac{1}{\tan 0°} = \frac{1}{0} = \text{not defined}$$

Consider Figure 6.2, which represents an angle of 90° (in standard position). **Just as in Figure 6.1, we cannot actually draw △OAB, since $\overline{AB}$ would lie on top of $\overline{OB}$.**

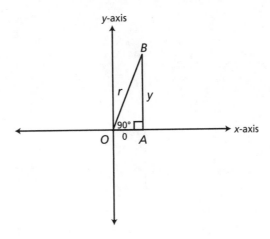

Figure 6.2

Using the Pythagorean theorem, $0^2 + y^2 = r^2$. Since y and r are both positive, this means that $y = r$. Notice that $x = 0$.

Here are the values of the six trigonometric ratios when $\theta = 90°$:

$$\sin 90° = \frac{y}{r} = \frac{r}{r} = 1$$

$$\cos 90° = \frac{0}{r} = 0$$

$$\tan 90° = \frac{y}{0} = \text{not defined}$$

$$\csc 90° = \frac{1}{\sin 90°} = \frac{1}{1} = 1$$

$$\sec 90° = \frac{1}{\cos 90°} = \frac{1}{0} = \text{not defined}$$

$$\cot 90° = \frac{0}{y} = 0$$

When a fraction is not defined, it means that the denominator is zero. Provided that the numerator is a nonzero quantity, the reciprocal of a nondefined fraction has a value of zero. For example, $\frac{7}{0}$ is not defined. Its reciprocal, $\frac{0}{7}$, has a value of zero.

Consider Figure 6.3, which represents an angle of **180°**, in standard position. Once again, **it is actually impossible to draw △AOB, since $\overline{OB}$ would lie on top of $\overline{OA}$.** We have to pull the $\overline{OA}$ up from the y-axis just so that you can see it! So, this is only a theoretical figure:

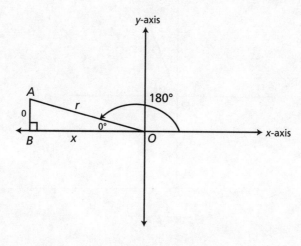

Figure 6.3

Using the Pythagorean theorem, $x^2 + 0^2 = r^2$.
Since $\overline{OA}$ lies on the negative section of the x-axis, this implies that x is negative while r is still positive.
Thus, $x = -r$. Notice that $y = 0$.

Here are the values of the six trigonometric ratios when $\theta = 180°$:

$$\sin 180° = \frac{0}{r} = 0$$

$$\cos 180° = \frac{x}{r} = \frac{-r}{r} = -1$$

$$\tan 180° = \frac{0}{x} = 0$$

$$\csc 180° = \frac{r}{0} = \text{not defined}$$

$$\sec 180° = \frac{1}{\cos 180°} = \frac{1}{-1} = -1$$

$$\cot 180° = \frac{1}{\tan 180°} = \frac{1}{0} = \text{not defined}$$

Consider Figure 6.4, which represents an angle of 270°, in standard position. As you can probably guess, it is impossible to draw $\triangle AOB$, since $\overline{AB}$ would lie on top of $\overline{OB}$. So again, we had to move $\overline{OA}$ away a bit from the y-axis so that we could see it.

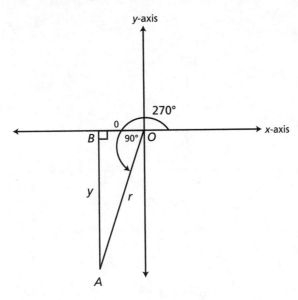

Figure 6.4

Using the Pythagorean theorem, $0^2 + y^2 = r^2$. Since $\overline{OA}$ lies on the negative section of the y-axis, this implies that y is negative while r is still positive. Thus, $y = -r$. Notice that $x = 0$.

Here are the values of the six trigonometric ratios when $\theta = 270°$:

$$\sin 270° = \frac{y}{r} = \frac{-r}{r} = -1$$

$$\cos 270° = \frac{0}{r} = 0$$

$$\tan 270° = \frac{y}{0} = \text{not defined}$$

$$\csc 270° = \frac{1}{\sin 270°} = \frac{1}{-1} = -1$$

$$\sec 270° = \frac{1}{\cos 270°} = \frac{1}{0} = \text{not defined}$$

$$\cot 270° = \frac{0}{y} = 0$$

Besides the quadrantal angles, there are a few **other "special" angles** for which the trigonometric ratios should be discussed in detail. Let's now review the properties of a 30°-60°-90° right triangle and a 45°-45°-90° right triangle.

Consider Figure 6.5, shown below.

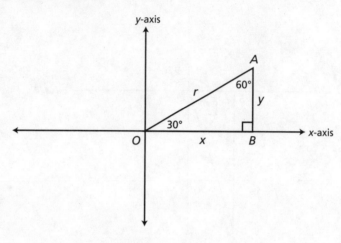

Figure 6.5

In any 30°-60°-90° right triangle, the length of the side opposite the 30-degree angle is exactly one half the length of the hypotenuse.

Since $y = \frac{1}{2} \times r$, $\sin 30° = \dfrac{\frac{1}{2}r}{r} = \dfrac{1}{2}$ or 0.5.

The relationship $y = \frac{1}{2} \times r$ can also be written as $r = 2y$.

Notice that the measure of $\angle A$ is 60°, because the two acute angles of any right triangle must add up to 90°.
The length of the side opposite the 60-degree angle is exactly the product of $\sqrt{3}$ and the length of the side opposite the 30-degree angle.
This means that $x = \left(\sqrt{3}\right)(y)$.

Since the sine value is always the ratio of the opposite side to the hypotenuse,

we can write: $\sin 60° = \dfrac{x}{r} = \dfrac{\sqrt{3}y}{2y} = \dfrac{\sqrt{3}}{2} \approx 0.8660$.

We can determine the value of cos 30° and cos 60° by using Figure 6.5.
Since the cosine value is always the ratio of the adjacent side to the hypotenuse,

$\cos 30° = \dfrac{x}{r} = \dfrac{\sqrt{3}y}{2y} = \dfrac{\sqrt{3}}{2} \approx 0.8660$ and $\cos 60° = \dfrac{y}{r} = \dfrac{\frac{1}{2}r}{r} = \dfrac{1}{2}$ or 0.5.

Notice that *sin 30° = cos 60° and that sin 60° = cos 30°. This is no accident! If θ is an acute angle, then sin θ = cos(90° − θ). If θ is not an acute angle, we need to find the measure of its corresponding reference angle. Note that we can also write cos θ = sin(90° − θ).*

1 Example: **In the fourth quadrant, the cosine of which angle has the same value as sin 112°?**

Solution: sin 112° = sin(180° − 112°) = sin 68°. Now sin 68° = cos 22°.
We need to find a fourth quadrant angle whose reference angle is 22°.
If we call this angle θ, then 360° − θ = 22°. Thus, θ = 338°.
As a check, the value of each of sin 112° and cos 338° is
approximately 0.9272.

2 Example: **In the third quadrant, the sine of which angle has the same value as cos 196°?**

Solution: cos 196° = cos(196° − 180°) = cos 16°. Now cos 16° = sin 74°.
We need to find a third quadrant angle whose reference angle is 74°.
If we call this angle θ, then θ − 74° = 180°. Thus, θ = 254°.

As a check, the value of each of cos 196° and sin 254° is
approximately −0.9613.

3 Example: **In the first quadrant, the cosine of which angle has the same**

value as $\sin \dfrac{\pi}{9}$ **radians ?**

Solution: The given angle is in radians, so we write $\sin \dfrac{\pi}{9} = \cos\left(\dfrac{\pi}{2} - \dfrac{\pi}{9}\right) = \cos \dfrac{7\pi}{18}$

radians. As a check, the value of each of $\sin \dfrac{\pi}{9}$ radians and

$\cos \dfrac{7\pi}{18}$ radians is approximately 0.3420.

Notice that we replaced 90° by $\dfrac{\pi}{2}$ radians.

Example: *In the fourth quadrant, the sine of which angle has the same value as cos 310°?*

Solution: If you are puzzled about this question, there is a very good reason. There is no answer! For any angle in the fourth quadrant, the sine value is <u>always</u> negative, and the cosine value is <u>always</u> positive. Hopefully, you were not fooled by this situation.

Let's return to the **30°-60°-90° right triangle**, as shown in Figure 6.5.

We discovered that $\sin 30° = \cos 60° = \dfrac{1}{2}$ and that $\sin 60° = \cos 30° = \dfrac{\sqrt{3}}{2} \approx 0.8660$.

Figure 6.6 shown below is a duplicate of Figure 6.5, with each of x, y, and r replaced by numbers.

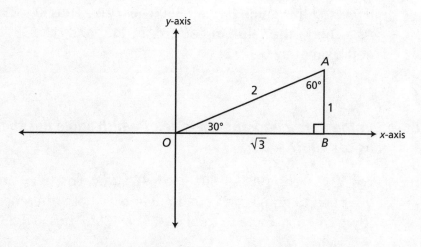

Figure 6.6

Since $\sin 30° = \dfrac{1}{2}$ and $\cos 30° = \dfrac{\sqrt{3}}{2}$, we can conveniently use the numbers 1, 2, and $\sqrt{3}$ to represent the sides of the right triangle.

Using this diagram and the definitions of the other four trigonometric ratios, we can conclude the following for each of 30° and 60°:

$$\tan 30° = \frac{1}{\sqrt{3}}$$

$$\tan 60° = \frac{\sqrt{3}}{1} = \sqrt{3}$$

$$\csc 30° = \frac{1}{\sin 30°} = \frac{1}{\frac{1}{2}} = 2$$

$$\csc 60° = \frac{1}{\sin 60°} = \frac{1}{\frac{\sqrt{3}}{2}} = \frac{2}{\sqrt{3}}$$

$$\sec 30° = \frac{1}{\cos 30°} = \frac{1}{\frac{\sqrt{3}}{2}} = \frac{2}{\sqrt{3}}$$

$$\sec 60° = \frac{1}{\cos 60°} = \frac{1}{\frac{1}{2}} = 2$$

$$\cot 30° = \frac{1}{\tan 30°} = \frac{1}{\frac{1}{\sqrt{3}}} = \sqrt{3}$$

$$\cot 60° = \frac{1}{\tan 60°} = \frac{1}{\sqrt{3}}$$

Each of these values can be verified with a calculator.

Another triangle with "special angles" is the **45°-45°-90° right triangle**, shown below in the first quadrant as Figure 6.7.

The assigned values of *OA, OB,* and *AB* are explained below.

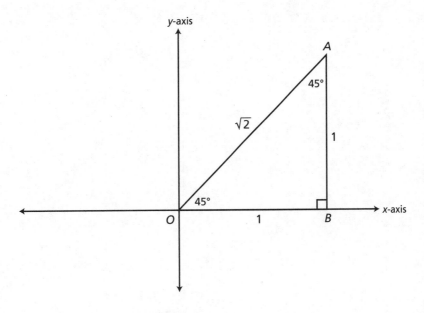

Figure 6.7

You can use your calculator to check that tan 45° = 1, which implies that $\frac{OB}{AB} = \frac{AB}{OB} = 1$.

Using the Pythagorean theorem, $1^2 + 1^2 = (OA)^2$. This equation simplifies to $(OA)^2 = 2$, so $OA = \sqrt{2}$.

Then the values of the six trigonometric ratios of 45° are as follows:

$$\sin 45° = \frac{1}{\sqrt{2}}$$

$$\cos 45° = \frac{1}{\sqrt{2}}$$

$$\tan 45° = 1$$

$$\csc 45° = \sqrt{2}$$

$$\sec 45° = \sqrt{2}$$

$$\cot 45° = 1$$

At this point, let's **summarize** the trigonometric ratios for all the quadrantal angles, as well as for 30°, 45°, and 60°. (Of course, each of these values can be verified with a calculator.) For those ratios that contain square roots, the calculator will yield the decimal equivalent.

	Sine	Cosine	Tangent	Cosecant	Secant	Cotangent
0°	0	1	0	not def.	1	not def.
30°	$\frac{1}{2}$	$\frac{\sqrt{3}}{2}$	$\frac{1}{\sqrt{3}}$	2	$\frac{2}{\sqrt{3}}$	$\sqrt{3}$
45°	$\frac{1}{\sqrt{2}}$	$\frac{1}{\sqrt{2}}$	1	$\sqrt{2}$	$\sqrt{2}$	1
60°	$\frac{\sqrt{3}}{2}$	$\frac{1}{2}$	$\sqrt{3}$	$\frac{2}{\sqrt{3}}$	2	$\frac{1}{\sqrt{3}}$
90°	1	0	not def.	1	not def.	0
180°	0	−1	0	not def.	−1	not def.
270°	−1	0	not def.	−1	not def.	0

Given an angle θ in the first quadrant, we can use the calculator to determine the value of any of the six trigonometric ratios.

For example, if θ = 22°, sin 22° ≈ 0.3746.

If $\theta = \frac{2\pi}{9}$ radians, $\tan \frac{2\pi}{9} \approx 0.8391$.

5 **Example:** *Besides 11°, determine an angle θ such that sin 11° = sin θ.*

Solution: We need to locate an angle greater than 90° such that its reference angle is 11°.
However, since sin 11° is a positive number, we are confined to the second quadrant.
The angle we are seeking is 180° − 11° = 169°.
As a check, sin 11° = sin 168° ≈ 0.1908.

6 **Example:** *Besides 48°, determine an angle θ such that cot 48° = cot θ.*

Solution: The cotangent ratio is positive in the first and third quadrants.
So, we need an angle in the third quadrant such that its reference angle is 48°. The correct angle is 180° + 48° = 228°.
As a check, cot 48° = cot 228° ≈ 0.9004.

If the given angle is in the second quadrant, our calculator will still show any of the six trigonometric ratio values. Of course, some of these will be negative numbers.

For example, if $\theta = \dfrac{3\pi}{5}$ radians, $\cos \dfrac{3\pi}{5} \approx -0.3090$. If $\theta = \dfrac{9\pi}{10}$ radians, $\cot \dfrac{9\pi}{10} \approx -3.0777$.

7 **Example:** *Besides $\dfrac{7\pi}{12}$ radians, determine an angle θ such that $\cos \dfrac{7\pi}{12} = \cos \theta$.*

Solution: Since $\dfrac{\pi}{2} < \dfrac{7\pi}{12} < \pi$, the angle $\dfrac{7\pi}{12}$ radians must lie in the second quadrant, where the cosine ratio is negative.

The corresponding reference angle is $\pi - \dfrac{7\pi}{12} = \dfrac{5\pi}{12}$.

Since the cosine ratio is also negative in the third quadrant, we seek a third-quadrant angle whose reference angle is $\dfrac{5\pi}{12}$ radians.

The correct angle is $\pi + \dfrac{5\pi}{12} = \dfrac{17\pi}{12}$ radians.

As a check, $\cos \dfrac{7\pi}{12} = \cos \dfrac{17\pi}{12} \approx -0.2588$.

8 **Example:** *Besides $\frac{7\pi}{8}$ radians, determine an angle θ such that $\csc\theta = \csc\frac{7\pi}{8}$.*

Solution: We know that $\frac{7\pi}{8}$ radians is in the second quadrant because

$\frac{\pi}{2} < \frac{7\pi}{8} < \pi$.

In the second quadrant, the cosecant ratio is positive.
The only other quadrant for which the cosecant ratio is positive is the first quadrant.
Thus, we only need to find the reference angle, which is

$\pi - \frac{7\pi}{8} = \frac{\pi}{8}$ radians. As a check, $\csc\frac{7\pi}{8} = \csc\frac{\pi}{8} \approx 2.6131$.

9 **Example:** *Given that sec 195° ≈ –1.0353, for which other angle is the secant ratio approximately equal to –1.0353?*

Solution: Although the wording is slightly different from the previous four examples, the meaning of the question is the same.
The secant ratio is negative in the second and third quadrants.
Since 195° is located in the third quadrant, we seek an angle in the second quadrant whose reference angle is the same as that for 195°. The reference angle for 195° is 15°.
Thus, the correct angle in the second quadrant is 180° – 15° = 165°.
As a check, we note that sec 165° ≈ –1.0353.

10 **Example:** *Given that $\tan\frac{9\pi}{5}$ rad ≈ –0.7265, for which other angle (in radian measure) is the tangent ratio approximately equal to –0.7265?*

Solution: The tangent ratio is negative in both the second and fourth quadrants.

Since $\frac{3\pi}{2} < \frac{9\pi}{5} < 2\pi$, we know that $\frac{9\pi}{5}$ radians is located in the fourth quadrant.

Its reference angle is $2\pi - \frac{9\pi}{5} = \frac{\pi}{5}$ radians.

We seek an angle in the second quadrant whose reference angle is $\frac{\pi}{5}$ radians.

The correct angle is $\pi - \frac{\pi}{5} = \frac{4\pi}{5}$ radians.

As a check, we note that $\frac{4\pi}{5} \approx -0.7265$.

Test Yourself!

1. The cosine of which acute angle has the same value as sin 56°?

   Answer: _____

2. Which one of the following has a value of −1?

   (A)   tan 270°   (C)   sin 90°

   (B)   csc 270°   (D)   cos 90°

3. Consider the following list of six trigonometric ratios, in which the angles are in radian measure:

   $$\sin \pi$$
   $$\cos 0$$
   $$\tan \frac{3\pi}{2}$$
   $$\csc \frac{\pi}{2}$$
   $$\sec \frac{\pi}{3}$$
   $$\cot \frac{\pi}{4}$$

   How many of these ratios are <u>not</u> defined?

   Answer: _____

4. Which one of the following has the same value as tan 45°?

   (A)   cos 45°   (C)   tan 90°

   (B)   sec 90°   (D)   cot 45°

5. Besides 62°, determine an angle θ such that sec 62° = sec θ.

   Answer: _____

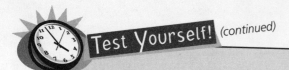

6.   Besides $\dfrac{7\pi}{4}$ radians, determine an angle θ (in radian measure)

      such that cot $\dfrac{7\pi}{4}$ = cot θ .

                                             Answer: _____

7.   How many of the six trigonometric ratios have a negative value in
      both the third and fourth quadrants?

                                             Answer: _____

8.   In the fourth quadrant, the sine of which angle has the same
      value as cos 97°?

                                             Answer: _____

9.   Given that csc $\dfrac{\pi}{15}$ ≈ 4.8097, for which other angle (in radian
      measure) is the cosecant ratio approximately equal to 4.8097?

                                             Answer: _____

10.   In the second quadrant, the cosine of which angle has the same
      value as sin 306°?

                                             Answer: _____

Inverse Trigonometric Values

In this lesson, we will explore the concept of **inverse trigonometric values**. As an example, we can easily check that $\sin 30° = \dfrac{1}{2}$. Instead of determining the value of $\sin 30°$, we will be asked to determine the angle(s) θ for which the trigonometric ratio is true.

Your Goal: When you have completed this lesson, you should be able to determine the angle (or angles) that match a given trigonometric ratio.

Inverse Trigonometric Values

If you are given $\sin \theta = \dfrac{1}{2}$, then from the introduction, you know that $\theta = 30°$ or $\dfrac{\pi}{6}$ radians. The statement $\sin 30° = \dfrac{1}{2}$ can also be written as $30° = \sin^{-1}\left(\dfrac{1}{2}\right)$, which is read as "30 degrees equals the **inverse** sine of one-half." Another equivalent statement would be "30 degrees equals the angle whose sine value is one-half." Using radians, we would write $\dfrac{\pi}{6} = \sin^{-1}\left(\dfrac{1}{2}\right)$. **The parentheses following the number after "sin⁻¹" are used only for ease of reading.**

Is there another angle whose value is $\sin^{-1}\left(\dfrac{1}{2}\right)$? Our answer must be yes, because the sine ratio is also positive in the second quadrant. We just need to find the angle in the second quadrant whose reference angle is 30°.

Our answer is $180° - 30° = 150°$. Thus, we can write $150° = \sin^{-1}\left(\dfrac{1}{2}\right)$.

In radian measure, this would appear as $\dfrac{5\pi}{6} = \sin^{-1}\left(\dfrac{1}{2}\right)$.

Be sure you realize that $\sin^{-1}\left(\dfrac{1}{2}\right)$ does <u>not</u> equal $\dfrac{1}{\sin \frac{1}{2}}$. The expression $\dfrac{1}{\sin \frac{1}{2}}$ would mean the reciprocal of $\sin \dfrac{1}{2}$ radian.

Another popular expression for inverse ratios is using "arc" in front of the trigonometric ratio.

For example, $\sin^{-1}\left(\dfrac{1}{2}\right)$ can be written as $\arcsin \dfrac{1}{2}$.

1   **Example:**   *In degree measure, what are the values of* $\sin^{-1}\left(\dfrac{\sqrt{3}}{2}\right)$ *?*

Solution: Your calculator has buttons labeled as *sin⁻¹*, *tan⁻¹*, and *cos⁻¹*. First press the sin⁻¹ button. The display on your calculator will now appear as *sin⁻¹(*.

Now press the following buttons in sequence:

    1) $\sqrt{3}$
    2) a right parenthesis following the 3
    3) the division symbol
    4) the number 2
    5) then another right parenthesis

Your calculator display should now appear as "$\sin^{-1}\left(\sqrt{(3)} \div 2\right)$."
Finally, press *Enter* to get the answer: 60.

As long as your calculator is in "degree" mode, this means that the answer is 60°. But don't stop here!

The sine ratio is also positive in the second quadrant, for which the reference angle is 60°.
Therefore, another answer is 180 − 60 = 120°.

MathFlash!

On a TI 83 calculator, as soon as you press the square root key, a left parenthesis automatically appears. This is the reason why you must supply a right parenthesis following the 3. If you fail to provide this right parenthesis, your display will appear as $\sin^{-1}(\sqrt{3 \div 2}$.

At this point, even if you put in a right parenthesis after the 2, the calculator will show ERROR. The reason is because the calculator is trying to evaluate $\sin^{-1}\left(\sqrt{\dfrac{3}{2}}\right)$, *which has no value. You want to be certain that the number 2 is* <u>not</u> *under the square root symbol.*

2 **Example:**   *What are the values of* $\tan^{-1}\left(-\dfrac{1}{4}\right)$, *to the nearest degree?*

Solution: On your calculator, if you press the *tan⁻¹* button followed by $\left(-\dfrac{1}{4}\right)$, the result will read as approximately –14.

This means that the answer is –14°.
Since our workbook will only deal with positive angle measurements, we simply calculate 360° – 14° = 346°.
(Technically, an angle of –14° means that it has its initial ray on the *x*-axis and measures 14° in a <u>clockwise</u> direction.)
To get the second answer, we just need to find an angle in the second quadrant (where the tangent ratio is negative) that has a reference angle of 14°.
The correct answer is 180° – 14° = 166°.
As a check, notice that each of tan 346° and tan 166° has a value of approximately –0.2493.

This number is certainly very close to $-\dfrac{1}{4}$.

3 **Example:**   *What are the values of* cos⁻¹(0.33), *to the nearest degree?*

Solution: On your calculator, press the *cos⁻¹* button, followed by 0.33.
To the nearest integer, your answer is 71°.
Since the cosine ratio is also positive in the fourth quadrant, the second answer corresponds to the angle whose reference angle is 71°.
Therefore, the second answer is 360° – 71° = 289°.

4 **Example:**   *What are the values of* $\sec^{-1}\left(\dfrac{4}{3}\right)$, *to the nearest degree?*

Solution: Your calculator does not have an inverse secant button, so you might think that this example cannot be solved. Well, the good news is that there is a way to proceed!
We know that the secant ratio is the reciprocal of the cosine ratio.

So if the secant of an angle is $\dfrac{4}{3}$, it must be true that the cosine of that same angle is $\dfrac{3}{4}$, which is the reciprocal of $\dfrac{4}{3}$.

We need to find the values of $\cos^{-1}\left(\dfrac{3}{4}\right)$.

The calculator will give the first answer of 41°.
The second answer is found in the fourth quadrant, with a reference angle of 41°.
Thus, the second answer is 360° – 41° = 319°.

5   **Example:**   *What are the values of cot⁻¹(–1.56), to the nearest degree?*

Solution: Since the cotangent ratio is the reciprocal of the tangent ratio,

we can change $\cot^{-1}(-1.56)$ to $\tan^{-1}\left(-\dfrac{1}{1.56}\right)$.

We find that $\tan^{-1}\left(-\dfrac{1}{1.56}\right) \approx -33$, which means –33 °.

The angle measure that we want is 360° – 33° = 327°.
The second answer is in the second quadrant with a reference angle of 33°.
Thus, the second answer is 180° – 33° = 147°.

MathFlash!

In Example 5, we could have changed $-\dfrac{1}{1.56}$ to its approximate decimal equivalent of –0.641, but it is not necessary. The answers would still be 327° and 147°.

6   **Example:**   *To the nearest degree, for which third quadrant angle does its*

cosecant value equal $-\dfrac{11}{10}$?

Solution: This example is equivalent to asking for the value of $\csc^{-1}\left(-\dfrac{11}{10}\right)$,

for only the third quadrant angle.
The sine ratio is the reciprocal of the cosecant ratio, so we need

to determine $\sin^{-1}\left(-\dfrac{10}{11}\right)$.

The display on the calculator shows about –65 °.
If we were seeking the fourth quadrant angle, the answer would be 295°.
But, since we want the third quadrant angle, the correct answer is 180° + 65° = 245°.

As a quick check, $\csc 245° = \dfrac{1}{\sin 245°} \approx -1.1034$.

This number is very close to $-\dfrac{11}{10}$.

7 **Example:** *To the nearest degree, for which third quadrant angle does its cotangent value equal 0.321?*

Solution: We want the third quadrant angle whose value is $\cot^{-1}(0.321)$.

The first step is to change $\cot^{-1}(0.321)$ to $\tan^{-1}\left(\dfrac{1}{0.321}\right)$.

To the nearest degree, the calculator will display 72°.
This number becomes the reference angle for the actual answer of 180° + 72° = 252°.

8 **Example:** *Which one(s) of the following are <u>not</u> defined?*

$$\sin^{-1}(3)$$
$$\cos^{-1}(-0.95)$$
$$\tan^{-1}\left(\frac{3}{31}\right)$$
$$\csc^{-1}(-6)$$
$$\sec^{-1}\left(-\frac{12}{13}\right)$$
$$\cot^{-1}(0.08)$$

Solution: The only two of the above six inverse trigonometric ratios that are

not defined are $\sin^{-1}(3)$ and $\sec^{-1}\left(-\dfrac{12}{13}\right)$.

In the case of $\sin^{-1}(3)$, remember that the sine ratio is always the opposite side divided by the hypotenuse of a right triangle.
Since the hypotenuse is always the largest side, the sine ratio cannot exceed 1.

In the case of $\sec^{-1}\left(-\dfrac{12}{13}\right)$, the definition of a secant ratio is the

hypotenuse divided by the adjacent side in a right triangle.
Since the hypotenuse is the largest side, the secant ratio cannot be less than 1.
The other four selections have answers as follows (rounded off to the nearest degree):

$$\cos^{-1}(-0.95) = 162° \text{ and } 198°$$
$$\tan^{-1}\left(\frac{3}{31}\right) = 6° \text{ and } 186°$$
$$\csc^{-1}(-6) = 190° \text{ and } 350°$$
$$\cot^{-1}(0.08) = 85° \text{ and } 265°$$

As a **summary** of this lesson, the following statements are equivalent.

1. $\cos 60° = 0.5$

2. $60° = \cos^{-1}(0.5)$

3. $60° = \arccos(0.5)$

4. $60°$ represents an angle whose cosine ratio (or value) is 0.5.

In many practical applications involving trigonometric ratios, it is much simpler to use degree measure, rather than radian measure, for angles. <u>From this point forward, we will only use degree measures for angles.</u>

Test Yourself!

1. What are the values of $\tan^{-1}\left(\dfrac{5}{3}\right)$, to the nearest degree?

    Answers: _____

2. What are the values of $\cos^{-1}\left(-\dfrac{\sqrt{3}}{2}\right)$, to the nearest degree?

    Answers: _____

3. What are the values of $\csc^{-1}(2.65)$, to the nearest degree?

    Answers: _____

4. What are the values of $\sec^{-1}(-1.42)$, to the nearest degree?

    Answers: _____

Test Yourself! (continued)

5.   To the nearest degree, for which fourth quadrant angle does its cosine value equal $\frac{5}{9}$?

Answer: _____

6.   To the nearest degree, for which second quadrant angle does its cotangent value equal –0.38?

Answer: _____

7.   To the nearest degree, for which third quadrant angle does its sine value equal $-\frac{5}{16}$?

Answer: _____

8.   To the nearest degree, for which second quadrant angle does its cosecant value equal 1.85?

Answer: _____

9.   Which one of the following is <u>not</u> equivalent to tan 315° = –1?

(A)   tan(–1) = 315°

(B)   arctan(–1) = 315°

(C)   315° represents an angle whose tangent ratio is –1.

(D)   315° = tan^{-1}(–1)

10.   Which one of the following is <u>not</u> defined?

(A) $\cos^{-1}\left(\frac{2}{15}\right)$ (C)   sec^{-1}(–0.26)

(B) $\csc^{-1}\left(-\frac{11}{7}\right)$ (D)   cot^{-1}(1.36)

Solving Right Triangles—Part I

In this lesson, we will explore the methods used to solve for either of the **two acute angles** or any of the **three sides of a right triangle**. All the sides will be given in the same units, and all the angles will be given in degree measure. We will also discover what is the minimum amount of information needed in order to find the values of all sides and angles.

Your Goal: When you have completed this lesson, you should be able to determine the value of any unknown side or angle.

LESSON 8

Solving Right Triangles—Part 1

Our model triangle that will be used will be $\triangle ABC$, with the following designations:

1. The length of $\overline{BC}$ will be represented as a. This is one of the legs. It is located opposite $\angle A$.

2. The length of $\overline{AC}$ will be represented as b. This is also one of the legs. It is located opposite $\angle B$.

3. The length of $\overline{AB}$ will be represented as c. This is the hypotenuse, which is the longest side. It is located opposite $\angle C$, which is the right angle.

Figure 8.1, shown below, illustrates these features. Although it appears that $a > b$, do not assume that this is true. In other right triangles, it is possible that $a < b$ or that $a = b$.

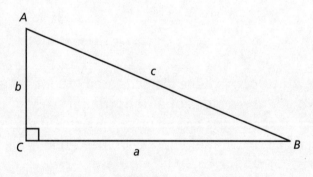

Figure 8.1

1 **Example:** *If a = 5 and b = 9, what is the value of c, to the nearest hundredth?*

Solution: Do you recognize this type of question from your geometry class? By the Pythagorean theorem, $c^2 = a^2 + b^2$. In this example, $c^2 = 5^2 + 9^2$. This means that $c^2 = 25 + 81 = 106$. Thus, $c = \sqrt{106} \approx 10.30$.

2 **Example:** *If a = 3.2 and c = 15, what is the value of b, to the nearest hundredth? (Use Figure 8.1 on page 92.)*

Solution: This is still the Pythagorean theorem, just dressed up in a different outfit! By substitution, $15^2 = (3.2)^2 + b^2$.
Then $b^2 = 15^2 - (3.2)^2 = 225 - 10.24 = 214.76$.
Thus, $b = \sqrt{214.76} \approx 14.65$.

3 **Example:** *If m∠A = 35° and c = 24, what is the value of a, to the nearest hundredth?*

Solution: You have already seen an example similar to this in Lesson 2. The diagram could appear as follows:

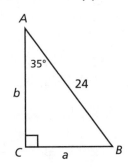

Since the sine ratio deals with the opposite side and the hypotenuse, by definition, $\sin 35° = \dfrac{a}{24}$.
Multiply both sides by 24 to get $a = (24)(\sin 35°) \approx 24 \times 0.5736 \approx 13.77$.

MathFlash!

The notation m∠A means "the measure of angle A."

---

4 **Example:** *Using the information and diagram from Example 3, what is the value of b to the nearest hundredth?*

Solution: Using the information that $a = 13.77$ and that $c = 24$, we can use the Pythagorean theorem.
$24^2 = (13.77)^2 + b^2$.
Then we get $b^2 = 576 - 189.6129 = 386.3871$.
Thus, $b = \sqrt{386.3871} \approx 19.66$.

On occasion, a problem may be solved in two different ways. We could have used the cosine ratio. By definition, $\cos 35° = \dfrac{b}{24}$. Then $b = (24)(\cos 35) \approx 19.66$. Either method will yield the same answer.

If you were asked to find $m\angle B$ from the diagram in Example 3, simply subtract 35° from 90° to get 55°. **Remember that the acute angles of any right triangle must add up to 90°.**

5   **Example:**   *If $a = 21$ and $b = 11$, what is the measure of $\angle B$ to the nearest degree? (Use Figure 8.1 on page 92.)*

Solution: Using the definition of the tangent ratio, we can write

$\tan \angle B = \dfrac{b}{a} = \dfrac{11}{21}$. Thus, $\angle B = \tan^{-1}\left(\dfrac{11}{21}\right) \approx 28°$.

Notice that we do <u>not</u> solve for a second answer, which would be found in the third quadrant, because any angle in the third quadrant would exceed 180°.

The cotangent ratio could also have been used in Example 5. The solution would have been found by calculating $\cot^{-1}\left(\dfrac{21}{11}\right)$.

6 **Example:** *If b = 7.5 and c = 40.2, what is the measure of ∠A to the nearest degree?*

Solution: Shown below is a diagram to assist you.

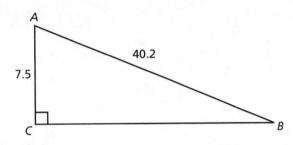

It should be evident that we will use the cosine ratio.

So, $\cos \angle A = \dfrac{7.5}{40.2}$. Thus, $\angle A = \cos^{-1}\left(\dfrac{7.5}{40.2}\right) \approx 79°$.

Here are some **word problem examples** involving trigonometric ratios.

7 **Example:** *A 30-foot vertical tree casts a 9-foot shadow on the ground, as shown in the diagram below.*

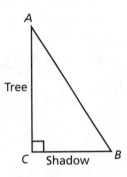

What is the measure of the angle of elevation from the end of the tree's shadow to the top of the tree? (to the nearest degree)

Solution: The angle of elevation corresponds to ∠B. Then $\tan \angle B = \dfrac{30}{9}$.

Thus, $\angle B = \tan^{-1}\left(\dfrac{30}{9}\right) \approx 73°$.

As we did with Example 5, we do <u>not</u> determine the angle in the third quadrant whose tangent ratio is $\dfrac{30}{9}$.

8   **Example:**   *Cheryl is standing at point A, which is on a bridge that is 150 feet above and parallel to the water. She is looking at a ship in the water, as shown in the diagram below.*

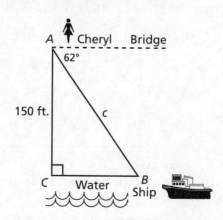

If the angle of depression is 62°, how many feet apart are Cheryl and this ship? (to the nearest hundredth of a foot)

Solution: Cheryl is at point *A*, while the ship is at point *B*.
The **angle of depression** is defined as the angle between the bridge and the imaginary line segment that would extend from Cheryl to the ship.

In geometry, you learned that alternate interior angles of parallel lines cut by a transversal have the same measure.
Therefore, $m\angle B = 62°$.
Since we need to find value of *c*, we can use the sine ratio.
Then, $\sin 62° = \dfrac{150}{c}$.

As we did in Lesson 2, multiply both sides of the equation by *c* to get $c \sin 62° = 150$.
Finally, $c = \dfrac{150}{\sin 62°} \approx 169.89$ feet.

MathFlash!

The angle of depression from point A in our right triangle ABC always has the same measure as the angle of elevation from point B.

9 **Example:** A 72-foot ladder is leaning against the side of a building, as shown below.

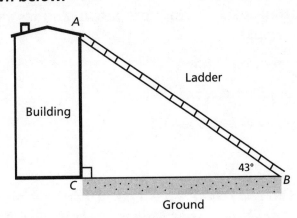

If the angle of elevation is 43°, then the bottom of the ladder is how many feet from the bottom of the building?

Solution: We need to find the value of *a*, so we will use the cosine ratio.

Then, $\cos 43° = \dfrac{a}{72}$.

Multiply both sides of the equation by 72 to get
$a = (72)(\cos 43°) \approx 52.66$ feet.

10 **Example:** A 32-foot wire is connected from the top of a vertical pole to a stake in the ground, as shown below.

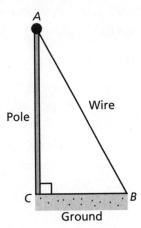

If the height of the pole is 28 feet, what is the measure of the angle between the wire and the pole? (to the nearest degree)

Solution: We need to find the measure of $\angle A$.

Using the cosine ratio, we can write $\cos \angle A = \dfrac{28}{32}$.

Thus, $\angle A = \cos^{-1}\left(\dfrac{28}{32}\right) \approx 29°$.

We will end this lesson with **two applications to rate, time, and distance,** as they relate to a right triangle. You may recall that distance equals rate times time. In symbols, this statement can be written as $D = RT$. Each of these quantities must be expressed in the same units. For our examples:

- distance is measured in miles

- rate is measured in miles per hour

- time is measured in hours

11   **Example:**   *Lou and Dawn leave a particular location, C, at the same time. Lou is walking east at 5 miles per hour, and Dawn is walking north at 3 miles per hour. A diagram is provided below.*

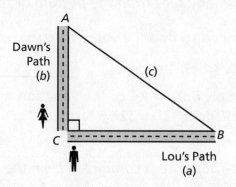

          How many miles apart are Lou and Dawn after 4 hours? (to the nearest hundredth of a mile)

Solution: The distance between Lou and Dawn is represented by c, which is $\overline{AB}$. The distance that Lou travels, represented by a, is $(5)(4) = 20$ miles. The distance that Dawn travels, represented by b, is $(3)(4) = 12$ miles.
Using the Pythagorean theorem,
$c^2 = 20^2 + 12^2 = 400 + 144 = 544$.
Thus, $c = \sqrt{544} \approx 23.32$ miles.

12   **Example:**   *Robyn and Charlie leave a dance club at the same time. Robyn drives east, and Charlie drives north. Robyn is driving at 45 miles per hour, and they are 290 miles apart after 5 hours. A diagram is provided below.*

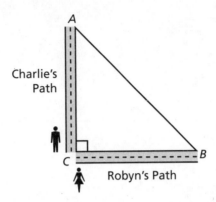

What is Charlie's speed in miles per hour? (to the nearest hundredth)

Solution: Let x represent Charlie's speed. Robyn's distance is $(45)(5) = 225$ miles. Charlie's distance is $5x$.
Using the Pythagorean theorem, $(5x)^2 + 225^2 = 290^2$.
Simplifying, we get $25x^2 + 50{,}625 = 84{,}100$. So $25x^2 = 33{,}475$, which leads to $x^2 = 1339$.
Thus, $x = \sqrt{1339} \approx 36.59$ miles per hour.

Be careful when calculating $(5x)^2$, which is $(5x)(5x)$.

Test Yourself!

For 1–4, use the following diagram.

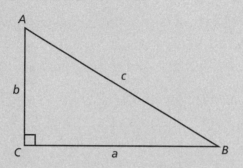

1.   If $b = 8.3$ and $c = 27$, what is the value
of a, to the nearest hundredth?   *Answer:* _____

2.   If $a = 11$ and $c = 17$, what is the measure
of $\angle A$, to the nearest degree?   *Answer:* _____

3.   If $b = 35$ and $m\angle B = 20°$, what is the
value of a, to the nearest hundredth?   *Answer:* _____

4.   If $c = 48.6$ and $m\angle A = 75°$, what is the
value of b, to the nearest hundredth?   *Answer:* _____

5.   A 45-foot flagpole casts a 65-foot shadow on the ground.
What is the measure of the angle of elevation from the end
of the flagpole's shadow to the top of the flagpole?
(to the nearest degree)

    Answer: _____

6.   A 56-foot ladder is leaning against the side of a building.
The bottom of the ladder is 25 feet from the bottom of the
building. What is the angle of elevation of the ladder?
(to the nearest degree)

    Answer: _____

Test Yourself! *(continued)*

7. A wire is connected from the top of a vertical telephone pole to a stake in the ground. The height of the telephone pole is 80 feet, and the angle of elevation of the wire is 36°. What is the length of the wire? (to the nearest hundredth of a foot)

Answer: _____

8. Vito is standing on the top of a vertical cliff near a lake. He is looking at a small boat in the lake that is 400 feet from the bottom of the cliff. If the angle of depression is 24°, what is the height of the cliff? (to the nearest hundredth of a foot)

Answer: _____

9. Jason and Melanie Brown leave their house at the same time. Jason is walking north at 3.5 miles per hour, while Melanie is walking at 5.5 miles per hour. How many miles apart are they after 3 hours? (to the nearest hundredth of a mile)

Answer: _____

10. Rachel and Jeff leave the post office at the same time. Rachel drives north at 52 miles per hour, while Jeff is driving east. After 2 hours, they are 160 miles apart. What is Jeff's speed in miles per hour? (to the nearest hundredth)

Answer: _____

Solving Right Triangles—Part 2

In this lesson, we will explore the methods used to solve for any **missing angles or sides of figures that contain two right triangles**. There are two distinct situations. Either (a) one of the triangles will be included in the other triangle or (b) the two triangles will share a common side. As in Lesson 8, all the sides will be given in the same units, and all the angles will be given in degree measure.

Your Goal: When you have completed this lesson, given sufficient information about the two given right triangles, you should be able to determine the value of any unknown side or angle.

Solving Right Triangles—Part 2

For the situation in which one triangle is included in the other triangle, the model we will use is shown below in Figure 9.1:

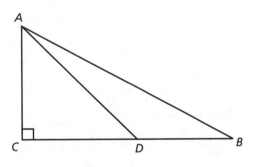

Figure 9.1

Here are the valid assumptions we can make:

1. $\angle C$ is the right angle for each of $\triangle ABC$ and $\triangle ADC$.

2. $\angle ADB$ is an obtuse angle, and all the other angles in the figure, except $\angle C$, are acute. Thus, $\angle ADB$ is the largest angle.

3. $AD > AC$, $AD > CD$, $AB > AC$, $AB > BC$, and $AB > AD$.

4. Of the five individual segments that connect any two adjacent points, $\overline{AB}$ is the largest. However, any of $\overline{AC}$, $\overline{CD}$, or $\overline{BD}$ may be the smallest.

1 **Example:** *If AC = 9, BC = 15, and BD = 8, what is the measure of ∠ADC? (to the nearest degree)*

Solution: The notation *AC* is used to represent the length of the line segment $\overline{AC}$. Here is the appropriate diagram, with the numerical values included.

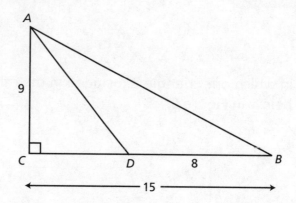

We can write *CB* = *CD* + *DB*.

By substitution, 15 = *CD* + 8, so *CD* = 7.

Using △*ADC*, $\tan \angle ADC = \dfrac{AC}{CD} = \dfrac{9}{7}$.

Thus, $\angle ADC = \tan^{-1}\left(\dfrac{9}{7}\right) \approx 52°$.

Even though the tangent ratio is positive in the third quadrant, remember that an angle of any triangle cannot exceed 180°.

2   **Example:**   *If AD = 20, m∠CAD = 30°, and BC = 28, what is the value of BD?*

Solution:

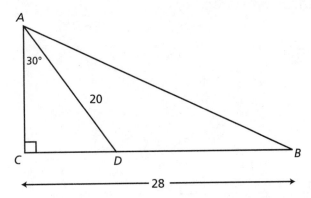

Triangle *ADC* is the key to determining the value of *BD*.

By the definition of the sine ratio, $\sin 30° = \dfrac{CD}{AD} = \dfrac{CD}{20}$.

Then $CD = (20)(\sin 30°) = 10$.
Finally, $BC - CD = BD$.
So, $28 - 10 = 18$.

3   **Example:**   *If BC = 40, m∠ADC = 75°, and m∠ABD = 54°, what is the value of AD? (to the nearest hundredth)*

Solution: We do not know the value of any of the sides in △*ACD*, so we must focus on △*ABC*. We want to solve for a side that belongs to both these triangles. This means that we need to find the value of *AC*.

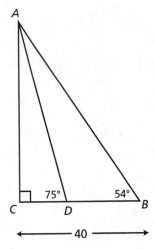

In △*ABC*, $\tan 54° = \dfrac{AC}{BC} = \dfrac{AC}{40}$.

Then $AC = (40)(\tan 54°) \approx 55.06$.

Now in △*ADC*, $\sin 75° = \dfrac{AC}{AD} = \dfrac{55.06}{AD}$.

This leads to $(AD)(\sin 75°) = 55.06$.

Thus, $AD = \dfrac{55.06}{\sin 75°} \approx 57.00$.

MathFlash!

In examples such as this one, it is important to develop a plan of attack. Otherwise, you will be traveling all around "Angle-wood" in search of the desired answer.

4   **Example:**   *If AC = 22, AD = 38, and DB = 15, what is the measure of ∠B?*
(to the nearest degree)

Solution:

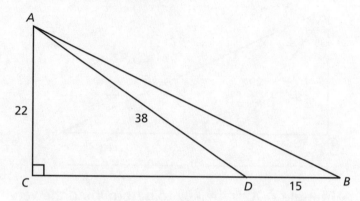

We will focus on △ADC, since we already know two of its sides.
By the Pythagorean theorem, $22^2 + (CD)^2 = 38^2$.
Then $(CD)^2 = 38^2 - 22^2 = 1444 - 484 = 960$.
So $CD = \sqrt{960} \approx 30.98$.
This means that $BC = 30.98 + 15 = 45.98$.

Now since $\tan \angle B = \dfrac{22}{45.98}$, $\angle B = \tan^{-1}\left(\dfrac{22}{45.98}\right) \approx 26°$.

5   **Example:**   *If CD = 6.2, DB = 16, and m∠ADB = 107°, what is the value of AB?*
(to the nearest hundredth)

Solution:

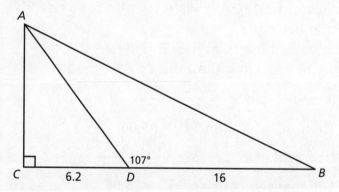

Immediately, we know that $m\angle ADC = 180° - 107° = 73°$.
We now need to determine an angle measure or the length of a
side in △ABC that will help us to find the value of AB.
The "wanted" side is $\overline{AC}$ because it lies in both △ADC and △ABC.

In △ADC, $\tan 73° = \dfrac{AC}{6.2}$.

This means $AC = (6.2)(\tan 73°) \approx 20.28$.
Using the Pythagorean theorem in △ABC, and noting that
$CB = 22.2$, we can write $(20.28)^2 + (22.2)^2 = (AB)^2$.
Then, $(AB)^2 \approx 411.28 + 492.84 = 904.12$.
Finally, $AB = \sqrt{904.12} \approx 30.07$.

6 **Example:**   *If AB = 56 and CD = 18, and m∠ABC = 22°, what is the measure of ∠CAD? (to the nearest degree)*

Solution:

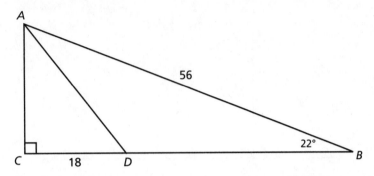

Our plan will be to first find any missing part of △ACD, other than ∠CAD.

Notice that $\overline{AC}$ belongs to both △CAD and △ABC.

In △ABC, $\sin 22° = \dfrac{AC}{56}$, so $AC = (56)(\sin 22°) \approx 20.98$.

Now we know two sides of △ACD.

Then $\tan \angle CAD = \dfrac{18}{20.98}$, which means that

$$\angle CAD = \tan^{-1}\left(\frac{18}{20.98}\right) \approx 41°.$$

Our **second model diagram** will show two right triangles with a common side. It is shown below as Figure 9.2:

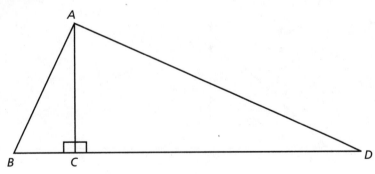

Figure 9.2

Here are the valid assumptions we can make:

1.   ∠C is the right angle for each of △ABC and △ADC.

2.   Each of ∠ABC, ∠ADC, ∠BAC, and ∠DAC is acute. However, ∠DAB may be acute, right, or obtuse.

3.   AD > AC, AD > CD, AB > AC, and AB > BC.

4.   △DAB may be a right triangle, an acute triangle, or an obtuse triangle.

5.   Although $\overline{BD}$ appears to be the largest segment of △DAB, this is not necessarily true. However, any of $\overline{AC}$, $\overline{BC}$, or $\overline{CD}$ may be the smallest segment.

7   **Example:**   *If AB = 8, BC = 5, and AD = 14, what is the measure of ∠CAD? (to the nearest degree)*

Solution:

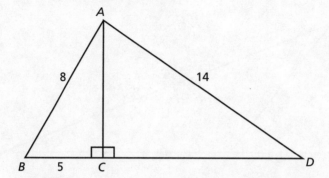

We need to first determine the remaining missing side of △ABC, which is $\overline{AC}$.

By the Pythagorean theorem, $5^2 + (AC)^2 = 8^2$.

Then $(AC)^2 = 8^2 - 5^2 = 64 - 25 = 39$.

This means that $AC = \sqrt{39} \approx 6.24$.

Now we know two sides of △ACD, so we can write $\cos \angle CAD = \dfrac{6.24}{14}$.

Finally, $\angle CAD = \cos^{-1}\left(\dfrac{6.24}{14}\right) \approx 64°$.

8   **Example:**   *If AB = 17, BD = 39, and m∠BAC = 48°, what is the value of CD? (to the nearest hundredth)*

Solution:

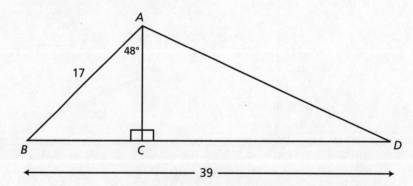

Since we already know that BD = 39, you can probably sense that we need to first find the value of BC.

Using △ABC, $\sin 48° = \dfrac{BC}{17}$.

Then $BC = (17)(\sin 48°) \approx 12.63$.

Thus, $CD = 39 - 12.63 = 26.37$.

9   **Example:**   *If BC = 20, CD = 15, and m∠ADC = 36°, what is the measure of ∠B?*
(to the nearest degree)

Solution:

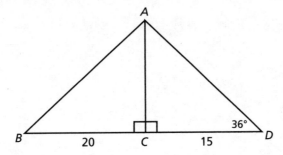

First, we will calculate the value of *AC*.

Using △*ACD*, $\tan 36° = \dfrac{AC}{15}$.

Then *AC* = (15)(tan 36°) ≈ 10.90.
Now use this value of *AC* in △*ABC*.

Since $\tan \angle B = \dfrac{10.90}{20}$, $\angle B = \tan^{-1}\left(\dfrac{10.90}{20}\right) \approx 29°$.

10   **Example:**   *If m∠B = 50°, m∠D = 27°, and AD = 44, what is the value of BC?*
(to the nearest hundredth)

Solution:

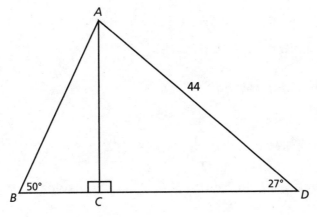

We will first find the value of *AC*.

In △*ACD*, $\sin 27° = \dfrac{AC}{44}$.

Then *AC* = (44)(sin 27°) ≈ 19.98.
Now we use this value of *AC* in △*ABC*.

Since $\tan 50° = \dfrac{19.98}{BC}$, this means that $BC = \dfrac{19.98}{\tan 50°} \approx \dfrac{19.98}{1.1918} \approx 16.76$.

Use the following diagram for 1–6.

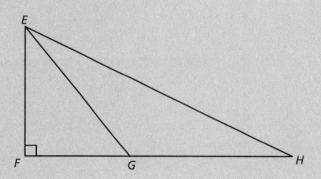

1.   If *FH* = 13, *EG* = 19, and *m∠FEG* = 40°,
      what is the value of *GH*?
      (to the nearest hundredth)   *Answer:* _____

2.   If *FG* = 9.5, *EH* = 23, and *m∠H* = 15°,
      what is the measure of *∠FEG*?
      (to the nearest degree)   *Answer:* _____

3.   If *EF* = 10, *EG* = 31, and *GH* = 16,
      what is the measure of *∠H*?
      (to the nearest degree)   *Answer:* _____

4.   If *FG* = 11, *GH* = 14, and *m∠EGH* = 125°,
      what is the value of *EH*?
      (to the nearest hundredth)   *Answer:* _____

5.   If *EF* = 21, *GH* = 12, and *EH* = 32,
      what is the measure of *∠EGH*?
      (to the nearest degree)   *Answer:* _____

6.   If *FH* = 60, *m∠EGF* = 66°, and *m∠H* = 39°,
      what is the value of *EG*?
      (to the nearest hundredth)   *Answer:* _____

 (continued)

Use the following diagram for 7–10.

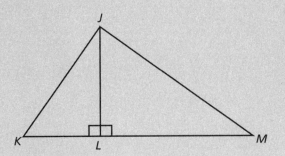

7. If *KL* = 7, *LM* = 28, and *m∠M* = 25°,
    what is the measure of ∠*K*?
    (to the nearest degree)   Answer: _____

8. If *JM* = 52, *m∠K* = 35°, and *m∠M* = 16°,
    what is the value of *KL*?
    (to the nearest hundredth)   Answer: _____

9. If *JK* = 55, *KM* = 64, and *m∠KJL* = 74°,
    what is the value of *LM*?
    (to the nearest hundredth)   Answer: _____

10. If *JK* = 30, *KL* = 19, and *JM* = 72,
    what is the measure of ∠*LJM*?
    (to the nearest degree)   Answer: _____

LESSONS
6-9

QUIZ TWO

1. **If θ represents an acute angle of any right triangle, then cos θ always has the same value as which one of the following?**

   A sin θ

   B cos(90° − θ)

   C sin(90° − θ)

   D cos(90° + θ)

2. **Consider the following figure that contains a right angle at *G*:**

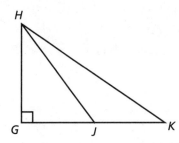

   If point *J* is any point on $\overline{GK}$, which one of the following statements is <u>not necessarily</u> true?

   A *GJ* > *JK*

   B *HJ* > *HG*

   C ∠*HJK* is an obtuse angle.

   D ∠*GHK* is an acute angle.

3. **Let *a*, *b*, and *c* represent the sides of a right triangle in which *c* is the hypotenuse.**
   If *a* = 5.4 and *c* = 10, then what is the value of *b*, to the nearest hundredth?

   A 11.36

   B 10.38

   C 9.40

   D 8.42

4. **To the nearest degree, what is the <u>larger</u> value of tan⁻¹(0.543)?**

   A 29°

   B 151°

   C 209°

   D 331°

5. **To the nearest degree, for which second quadrant angle does its secant value equal −2.6?**

   A 67°

   B 113°

   C 247°

   D 293°

6. **Consider the following figure, which contains a right angle at *Q*:**

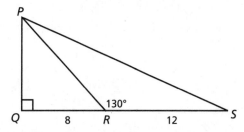

   What is the value of *PS* to the nearest hundredth?

   A 23.75

   B 22.95

   C 22.15

   D 21.35

7. Which one of the following is undefined?

   A csc π radians

   B cot $\frac{\pi}{2}$ radians

   C sin $\frac{\pi}{180}$ radians

   D cos $\frac{\pi}{3}$ radians

8. In the third quadrant, the sine of which angle has the same value as cos 215°?

   A 225°

   B 230°

   C 235°

   D 240°

9. A 75-foot ladder is leaning against the side of a building. The top of the ladder reaches a place on the building that is 40 feet above the ground. What is the angle of elevation of the ladder to the nearest degree?

   A 32°

   B 44°

   C 50°

   D 58°

10. Consider the following diagram in which the measure of ∠C = 90°.

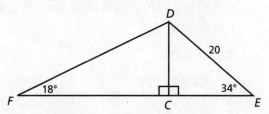

   What is the value of *FC* to the nearest hundredth?

   A 37.78

   B 34.41

   C 31.04

   D 27.67

Solving Oblique Triangles—Part I

In this lesson, you will be introduced to the methods used to **solve for any missing angles or sides of a triangle that contains no right angle**. Any triangle contains six "parts," namely, three sides and three angles. If we are given sufficient information about three parts, then we can solve for the values of the remaining parts of the triangle.

Your Goal: When you have completed this lesson, you should be able to solve for any missing part of an oblique triangle, given certain specific values.

Solving Oblique Triangles—Part 1

Let's return to Example 10 from Lesson 9, renamed below as Figure 10.1.

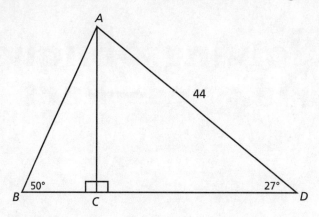

Figure 10.1

Suppose we had wanted to find the value of *AB*.
Using the value of the measure of ∠*B* (50°) and the answer we found for *BC* (16.76), we can find *AB* by using the cosine ratio.

$\text{Cos } 50° = \dfrac{16.76}{AB}$, which means that $AB = \dfrac{16.76}{\cos 50°} \approx 26.07$.

But suppose we did not have $\overline{AC}$ in our diagram. We would have △*ABD*, with no right angle. An **oblique** triangle is one that does not have a right angle.
Figure 10.2, shown below, is a duplicate of Figure 10.1 without $\overline{AC}$.

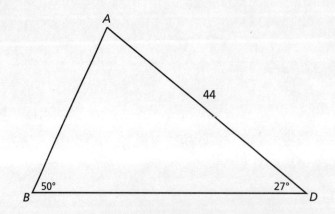

Figure 10.2

We have seen the number of steps required to find the value of *AB* when $\overline{AC}$ is given, (creating two right triangles). You are probably wondering if there is an easier way to calculate *AB*. The good news is that there is a proportion, called the Law of Sines, that will provide the answer to that question.

The **Law of Sines** states that given any triangle with sides labeled as *a*, *b*, and *c*, along with the angles opposite these respective sides labeled as $\angle A$, $\angle B$, and $\angle C$, the following proportion holds: $\dfrac{a}{\sin \angle A} = \dfrac{b}{\sin \angle B} = \dfrac{c}{\sin \angle C}$.

Look at $\triangle ABC$ shown in Figure 10.3 below.

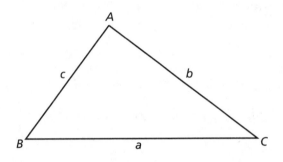

Figure 10.3

As stated in the Law of Sines, we have taken the liberty of labeling $\overline{BC}$ as *a*, $\overline{AC}$ as *b*, and $\overline{AB}$ as *c*. This labeling convention is commonly used because it helps in remembering this law.

MathFlash!

Even though the Law of Sines involves three fractions, only two of them are used at the same time. It is also possible to express the Law of Sines by using the reciprocals of each fraction. Thus, we can also write $\dfrac{\sin \angle A}{a} = \dfrac{\sin \angle B}{b} = \dfrac{\sin \angle C}{c}$.

Returning to Figure 10.2, we can solve for *AB* by using the proportion $\dfrac{AB}{\sin 27°} = \dfrac{44}{\sin 50°}$.
Cross-multiply to get $(AB)(\sin 50°) = (44)(\sin 27°) \approx 19.98$.

Thus, $AB = \dfrac{19.98}{\sin 50°} \approx 26.08$.

By checking the calculation below Figure 10.1, you can see that the "error" is only 0.01.
This error is due only to the rounding process.

1 **Example:** *In △ABC, if a = 12, m∠A = 41°, and m∠B = 75°, what is the value of b? (to the nearest hundredth)*

Solution: The diagram could appear as follows.

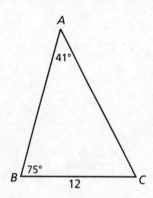

Then $\dfrac{12}{\sin 41°} = \dfrac{b}{\sin 75°}$.

Cross-multiply to get $(b)(\sin 41°) = (12)(\sin 75°) \approx 11.59$.

Thus, $b = \dfrac{11.59}{\sin 41°} \approx 17.67$.

2 **Example:** *Using the information in Example 1, what is the value of c? (to the nearest hundredth)*

Solution: At first glance, it appears that this is impossible because we do not have the measure of ∠C.

But, we know that the sum of the measures of the angles of any triangle is 180°.

Thus, $m∠C = 180° − 41° − 75° = 64°$.

Using the proportion $\dfrac{a}{\sin ∠A} = \dfrac{c}{\sin ∠C}$, we have $\dfrac{12}{\sin 41°} = \dfrac{c}{\sin 64°}$.

This leads to $(c)(\sin 41°) = (12)(\sin 64°) \approx 10.79$.

Thus, $c = \dfrac{10.79}{\sin 41°} \approx 16.45$.

There is a quick (and painless!) way to check whether this value of c is plausible. In your study of geometry, you learned that within any one triangle, the largest side is always opposite the largest angle. Also, the smallest side is always opposite the smallest angle. Look at the values of all three angles and all three sides from Examples 1 and 2, to verify this information.

3 **Example:** *In △DEF, DF = 26, m∠E = 43°, and m∠F = 32°. What is the value of DE? (to the nearest hundredth)*

Solution: Here is an appropriate diagram.

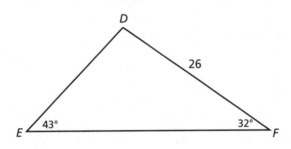

Then $\dfrac{26}{\sin 43°} = \dfrac{DE}{\sin 32°}$.

This leads to $(\sin 43°)(DE) = (26)(\sin 32°) \approx 13.78$.

Thus, $DE = \dfrac{13.78}{\sin 43°} \approx 20.21$.

4 **Example:** *Using the information in Example 3, what is the value of EF? (to the nearest hundredth)*

Solution: We actually have a choice of two different ratios in using the Law of Sines. Let's first use the proportion $\dfrac{EF}{\sin \angle D} = \dfrac{DF}{\sin \angle E}$.

In order to use the Law of Sines, we first need to find the measure of ∠D. From the given information, $m∠D = 180° - 43° - 32° = 105°$.

By substitution, $\dfrac{EF}{\sin 105°} = \dfrac{26}{\sin 43°}$.

Then $(EF)(\sin 43°) = (26)(\sin 105°) \approx 25.11$.

Thus, $EF = \dfrac{25.11}{\sin 43°} \approx 36.82$.

MathFlash!

The other proportion that could be used in determining the value of EF is $\dfrac{EF}{\sin \angle D} = \dfrac{DE}{\sin \angle F}$.

By substitution, this proportion becomes $\dfrac{EF}{\sin 105°} = \dfrac{20.21}{\sin 32°}$.

In solving this proportion, the value of EF will be approximately 36.84.

The difference of 0.02 in the two answers for EF is strictly the result of rounding off.

5 **Example:** *In $\triangle GHJ$, HJ = 20, $m\angle H = 50°$, and $m\angle J = 62°$. What is the value of GJ? (to the nearest hundredth)*

Solution: Here is an appropriate diagram.

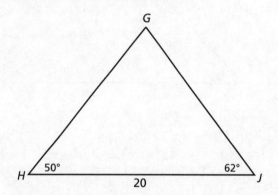

We will need the measure of $\angle G$, which is $180° - 50° - 62° = 68°$.

By the Law of Sines, $\dfrac{20}{\sin 68°} = \dfrac{GJ}{\sin 50°}$.

Then we cross-multiply to get $(GJ)(\sin 68°) = (20)(\sin 50°) \approx 15.32$.

Thus, $GJ = \dfrac{15.32}{\sin 68°} \approx 16.52$.

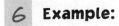 **Example:** *Consider the following triangle, in which each of the sides is marked as a single letter.*

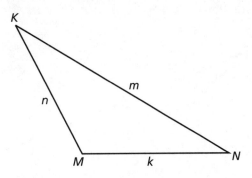

If n = 30, m∠K = 25°, and m∠M = 118°, what is the value of m? (to the nearest hundredth)

Solution: We first find that $m\angle N = 180° - 25° - 118° = 37°$.

By the Law of Sines, $\dfrac{m}{\sin 118°} = \dfrac{30}{\sin 37°}$.

Then $(m)(\sin 37°) = (30)(\sin 118°) \approx 26.49$.

Thus, $m = \dfrac{26.49}{\sin 37°} \approx 44.02$.

Up until now, we have been able to solve for a missing side of an oblique triangle when we are given the value of one side and the measures of any two angles. Let's examine an example that uses the **Law of Sines**, in which we are **given the lengths of two sides and the measure of an angle opposite one of these sides**.

7 **Example:** *In △PQR, PQ = 19, PR = 25, and m∠R = 20°. Given that ∠Q is an obtuse angle, what is the measure of ∠Q? (to the nearest degree)*

Solution: Let's draw an appropriate diagram, as shown below.

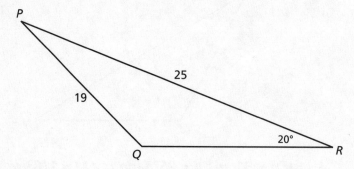

We immediately notice that *PQ* is opposite ∠*R*, and that *PR* is opposite ∠*Q*.

Using the Law of Sines, $\dfrac{19}{\sin 20°} = \dfrac{25}{\sin \angle Q}$.

Cross-multiplying, we get (19)(sin ∠Q) = (25)(sin 20°) ≈ 8.55.

Then we know that $\angle Q = \sin^{-1}\left(\dfrac{8.55}{19}\right)$.

At this point, we would normally just press the inverse sine button followed by the fraction $\dfrac{8.55}{19}$ and just round off the answer to the nearest degree. But, we would be absolutely wrong because your calculator will only reveal <u>an acute angle answer</u> of approximately 27°. You recall that the sine ratio is positive in <u>both</u> the first and second quadrants. Since we are given the fact that ∠Q is an <u>obtuse angle</u>, we must find the <u>second</u> quadrant angle for which the reference angle is 27°. Thus, the correct answer for the measure of ∠Q is 180° − 27° = 153°.

Incidentally, if we were given the information that ∠Q is acute, then the correct answer would be 27°. The appropriate diagram would have been as follows.

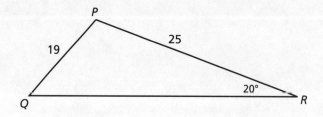

MathFlash!

If you are given the lengths of two sides of an oblique triangle and the measure of an angle opposite one of them, you need to be extra careful in solving for the missing angle opposite a known side. If we were not given any information about the size of $\angle Q$, then this example would have had two acceptable solutions. Some textbooks call this the "Side-Side-Angle" ambiguous case of the Law of Sines. There are also examples of "Side-Side-Angle" in which no possible solution exists. In this workbook, we will avoid examples of triangles with no solution.

In some cases, it is clear that only one answer will work, even when given we are given the "Side-Side-Angle" situation, as shown in Example 8.

8 **Example:** *In △STU, ST = 15, TU = 36, and m ∠S = 80°. What is the measure of ∠U? (to the nearest degree)*

Solution: First draw an appropriate diagram, as shown below.

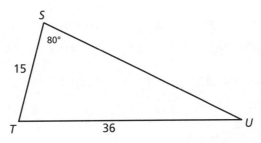

Using the Law of Sines, we can write $\dfrac{15}{\sin \angle U} = \dfrac{36}{\sin 80°}$.

Cross-multiply to get $(36)(\sin \angle U) = (15)(\sin 80°) \approx 14.77$.

Then $\sin \angle U = \dfrac{14.77}{36}$.

This leads to $\angle U = \sin^{-1}\left(\dfrac{14.77}{36}\right)$.

At this point, exactly one of 24° or 156° will be the correct answer.

There are two good reasons why the correct answer must be 24°:

(a)   Within one triangle, the larger the side, the larger the angle opposite that side. Since 36 > 15, $m\angle S > m\angle U$.

(b)   If the answer were 156°, then the sum of the angle measures at S and U would be 236°, which would exceed 180°.

9 **Example:** *Consider the following triangle, in which each of the sides is marked as a single letter.*

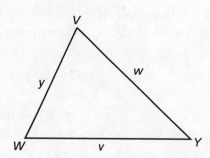

If v = 15, y = 10, and m ∠V = 68°, what is the measure of ∠W?

Solution: First, we will need to calculate the measure of ∠Y.

By the Law of Sines, $\dfrac{15}{\sin 68°} = \dfrac{10}{\sin \angle Y}$.

Then $(15)(\sin \angle Y) = (10)(\sin 68°) \approx 9.27$.

This means that $\sin \angle Y = \dfrac{9.27}{15}$, so that $\angle Y = \sin^{-1}\left(\dfrac{9.27}{15}\right) \approx 38°$.

Finally, the measure of $\angle W = 180° - 68° - 38° = 74°$.

10 **Example:** *In △ACE, CE = 27, AE = 57, and m∠A = 18°. Given that ∠C is an obtuse angle, what is the measure of ∠E?*

Solution: Let's draw an appropriate diagram.

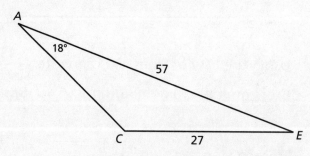

We will first need to calculate the measure of ∠C.

By the Law of Sines, $\dfrac{57}{\sin \angle C} = \dfrac{27}{\sin 18°}$.

Then $(27)(\sin \angle C) = (57)(\sin 18°) \approx 17.61$.

This implies that $\sin \angle C = \dfrac{17.61}{27}$, so that $\angle C = \sin^{-1}\left(\dfrac{17.61}{27}\right)$.

Since ∠C is obtuse, its measure must be 139°.

Finally, the measure of ∠E is $180° - 18° - 139° = 23°$.

If we were given no information concerning the size of ∠C, its measure could have been either 139° or 41°. Thus, there would have been two possible answers for the measure of ∠E. Besides 23°, the second answer would be 180° − 18° − 41° = 121°.

In **summary**, we can use the Law of Sines to find a missing side or missing angle, provided that we know the values of the following:

    (a) Two angles and any side, in order to find a second side

    (b) Two sides and a nonincluded angle, in order to find a second angle

In the case of (b), proceed with caution when you are seeking the measure of the second angle. Always check to be certain that larger angles lie opposite larger sides.

Use the following diagram for 1–4.
<u>Each problem is independent</u> of the others.

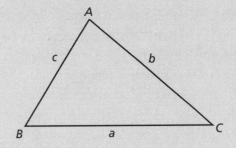

1.   If $a = 27$, $m\angle B = 48°$, and $m\angle C = 34°$,
        what is the value of c?
        (to the nearest hundredth)   *Answer:* _____

2.   If $b = 30$, $m\angle A = 73°$, and $m\angle B = 32°$,
        what is the value of a?
        (to the nearest hundredth)   *Answer:* _____

Test Yourself! (continued)

3.   If $a = 12$, $c = 19$, and $m\angle C = 65°$,
        what is the measure of $\angle A$?
        (to the nearest degree)   Answer: _____

4.   If $a = 42$, $b = 33$, and $m\angle A = 108°$,
        what is the measure of $\angle C$?
        (to the nearest degree)   Answer: _____

5.   In $\triangle DGJ$, $GJ = 16$, $m\angle D = 85°$, and
        $m\angle G = 56°$. What is the value of DJ?
        (to the nearest hundredth)   Answer: _____

6.   In $\triangle KMP$, $KM = 75$, $m\angle M = 25°$, and
        $m\angle P = 122°$. What is the value of MP?
        (to the nearest hundredth)   Answer: _____

7.   In $\triangle QSV$, $QS = 21$, $QV = 28$, and
        $m\angle S = 83°$. What is the measure
        of $\angle Q$? (to the nearest degree)   Answer: _____

8.   In $\triangle ZBD$, $ZB = 39$, $BD = 48$, and
        $m\angle D = 12°$. Given that $\angle Z$ is an
        obtuse angle, what is the measure
        of $\angle Z$? (to the nearest degree)   Answer: _____

9.   In $\triangle EGK$, $GK = 22$, $m\angle G = 76°$, and
        $m\angle K = 23°$. What is the value of EK?
        (to the nearest hundredth)   Answer: _____

10.   In $\triangle NPR$, $PR = 20$, $NR = 70$, and
        $m\angle P = 152°$. What is the measure
        of $\angle N$? (to the nearest degree)   Answer: _____

Solving Oblique Triangles—Part 2

In this lesson, we will explore additional methods used to solve for any **missing angles** or **sides** of an **oblique triangle**, when we are given either (a) the lengths of all sides or (b) the lengths of two sides and the measure of the included angle.

Your Goal: When you have completed this lesson, you should be able to solve for any missing part of an oblique triangle, given sufficient information about the known parts.

LESSON 11

Solving Oblique Triangles—Part 2

Up to this point, we have been able to establish the length of an unknown side or the measure of an unknown angle by using the Law of Sines. We had to have either:

(a) the measures of two angles and the length of any side, or

(b) the length of two sides and the measure of a non-included angle.

We now discuss the situation involving **two sides** and an **included angle**, which <u>cannot</u> be resolved with the Law of Sines.

Look at △ABC shown in Figure 11.1 below.

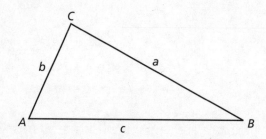

Figure 11.1

The **Law of Cosines** states that given any triangle labeled as shown in Figure 11.1, the following three equations apply:

(1) $a^2 = b^2 + c^2 - (2bc)(\cos \angle A)$

(2) $b^2 = a^2 + c^2 - (2ac)(\cos \angle B)$

(3) $c^2 = a^2 + b^2 - (2ab)(\cos \angle C)$

(These formulas look very similar to, but more expanded than, the Pythagorean theorem that you learned in geometry. You recall that theorem as $c^2 = a^2 + b^2$.)

1 **Example:** *Using Figure 11.1, if a = 16, c = 28, and m∠B = 45°, what is the value of b? (to the nearest hundredth)*

Solution: Use equation (2), since we seek the value of b:
$b^2 = a^2 + c^2 - (2ac)(\cos \angle B)$.
By substitution, $b^2 = 16^2 + 28^2 - (2)(16)(28)(\cos 45°)$.
This equation simplifies to $b^2 = 256 + 784 - (896)(0.7071) \approx 406.44$.
Thus, $b = \sqrt{406.44} \approx 20.16$.

2 **Example:** *Using Figure 11.1, if b = 41, c = 34, and m∠A = 111°, what if the value of a? (to the nearest hundredth)*

Solution: Use equation (1), since we seek the value of a:
$a^2 = b^2 + c^2 - (2bc)(\cos \angle A)$
By substitution, $a^2 = 41^2 + 34^2 - (2)(41)(34)(\cos 111°)$.
This equation simplifies to $a^2 = 1681 + 1156 - (2788)(-0.3584) \approx 3836.22$.
Thus, $a = \sqrt{3836.22} \approx 61.94$.

MathFlash!

A calculation such as (2)(41)(34)(cos 111°) can be done with one continuous multiplication, without first rounding off cos 111° (−0.3584) to the nearest ten-thousandth. The answers you get by using either method are almost identical.

We now discuss the **situation** in which we **know** the **lengths** of each of the **three sides**. The cosine formulas can be used to solve for the measure of any of the angles.

3 **Example:** *Using Figure 11.1, if a = 23, b = 8, and c = 21, what is the value of ∠B? (to the nearest degree)*

Solution: Our best bet is to select equation (2), since it involves ∠B.
By substitution, $8^2 = 23^2 + 21^2 - (2)(23)(21)(\cos \angle B)$.
This equation simplifies to $64 = 529 + 441 - (966)(\cos \angle B)$.
Then $-906 = (-966)(\cos \angle B)$.
Since $\cos \angle B = \dfrac{906}{966}$, $\angle B = \cos^{-1}\left(\dfrac{906}{966}\right) \approx 20°$.

4 **Example:** *Using Figure 11.1, if a = 9, b = 30, and c = 36, what is the value of ∠C? (to the nearest degree)*

Solution: We will use equation (3), since it involves ∠C.
By substitution, $36^2 = 9^2 + 30^2 - (2)(9)(30)(\cos \angle C)$.
This equation simplifies to $1296 = 81 + 900 - (540)(\cos \angle C)$.
Then $315 = (-540)(\cos \angle C)$.
Since $\cos \angle C = -\dfrac{315}{540}$, $\angle C = \cos^{-1}\left(-\dfrac{315}{540}\right) \approx 126°$.

MathFlash!

Notice that in Example 3, we took the inverse cosine of a _positive_ ratio, so the measure of the angle was found in the first quadrant. In Example 4, since the cosine ratio was _negative_, the measure of the angle was found in the second quadrant. Your calculator will automatically display the correct angle measure when you press the "cos⁻¹" button.

5 **Example:** *Using the information from Example 4, what is the measure of $\angle A$?*

Solution: Using the Law of Cosines, equation (1), we can write
$9^2 = 30^2 + 36^2 - (2)(30)(36)(\cos \angle A)$.
This equation simplifies to $81 = 900 + 1296 - (2160)(\cos \angle A)$.
Then $-2115 = (-2160)(\cos \angle A)$.
Since $\cos \angle A = \dfrac{2115}{2160}$, $\angle A = \cos^{-1}\left(\dfrac{2115}{2160}\right) \approx 12°$.

MathFlash!

Did you sense that another formula could have been used in solving for $\angle A$ in Example 5? Since we know the values of a, c, and $\angle C$, we could have used the Law of Sines.

Our solution would have started as $\dfrac{a}{\sin \angle A} = \dfrac{c}{\sin \angle C}$.

Then, by substitution, $\dfrac{9}{\sin \angle A} = \dfrac{36}{\sin 126°}$.

Cross-multiply to get $(36)(\sin \angle A) = (9)(\sin 126°) \approx 7.28$.

Finally, $\angle A = \sin^{-1}\left(\dfrac{7.28}{36}\right) \approx 12°$.

Our answers match, regardless of the method used.

As we saw in Lesson 10, there are many occasions in which the lettering of the triangle is different from *A*, *B*, and *C*. The same principles apply when you solve for the unknown side or angle. For ease of understanding, use a diagram.

6 **Example:**   *In △DFH, DH = 25, FH = 40, and m∠H = 33°. What is the value of DF? (to the nearest hundredth)*

Solution: The diagram shown below assists us in creating the appropriate equation that uses the Law of Cosines.

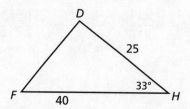

Since we know two sides and an included angle, we can write $(DF)^2 = (FH)^2 + (DH)^2 - (2)(FH)(DH)(\cos \angle H)$.
By substitution, $(DF)^2 = 40^2 + 25^2 - (2)(40)(25)(\cos 33°)$.
This equation simplifies to
$(DF)^2 = 1600 + 625 - (2000)(0.8387) = 547.6$.

Thus, $DF = \sqrt{547.6} \approx 23.40$.

7 **Example:**   *In △JLM, JL = 10, LM = 34, and m∠L = 127°. What is the value of JM? (to the nearest hundredth)*

Solution: Below is a diagram to help us.

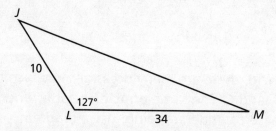

We know two sides and an included angle, so we can write $(JM)^2 = (JL)^2 + (LM)^2 - (2)(JL)(LM)(\cos \angle L)$.
By substitution, $(JM)^2 = 10^2 + 34^2 - (2)(10)(34)(\cos 127°)$.
Simplifying, we get
$(JM)^2 = 100 + 1156 - (680)(-0.6018) \approx 1665.22$.

Thus, $JM = \sqrt{1665.22} \approx 40.81$.

MathFlash!

If you are given the lengths of two sides and an included angle but are seeking the value of a second angle, you must first find the value of the unknown side. In Example 7, if you were asked to find the measure of ∠M, it would still have been necessary to first find the value of JM. Then you could have used either the Law of Sines or the Law of Cosines to complete the problem.

8 **Example:** *In △PRT, PR = 16, RT = 7, and PT = 20. What is the measure of ∠R? (to the nearest degree)*

Solution: The appropriate diagram appears below. (Since *PT* is only slightly larger than the sum of *PR* and *RT*, we can assume that ∠R is obtuse. If this assumption is incorrect, the problem can still be solved.)

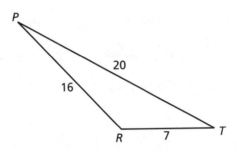

$(PT)^2 = (PR)^2 + (RT)^2 - (2)(PR)(RT)(\cos \angle R)$.
By substitution, $20^2 = 16^2 + 7^2 - (2)(16)(7)(\cos \angle R)$.
Simplifying, we get $400 = 256 + 49 - (224)(\cos \angle R)$.
This leads to $95 = (-224)(\cos \angle R)$.
Since $\cos \angle R = -\dfrac{95}{224}$, $\angle R = \cos^{-1}\left(-\dfrac{95}{224}\right) \approx 115°$.

MathFlash!

In using the Law of Cosines with three known sides, the left side of the equation should always represent the side opposite from the angle whose measure we are trying to find.

9 **Example:** *In △UVW, UV = 23, VW = 28, and UW = 19. What is the measure of ∠W? (to the nearest degree)*

Solution: Here is the diagram.

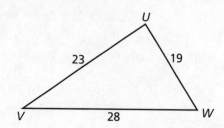

$(UV)^2 = (VW)^2 + (UW)^2 - (2)(VW)(UW)(\cos \angle W)$.
By substitution, $23^2 = 28^2 + 19^2 - (2)(28)(19)(\cos \angle W)$.
Simplifying, we get $529 = 784 + 361 - (1064)(\cos \angle W)$.
Then $-616 = (-1064)(\cos \angle W)$.

Since $\cos \angle W = \dfrac{616}{1064}$, $\angle W = \cos^{-1}\left(\dfrac{616}{1064}\right) \approx 55°$.

An interesting application of using the known sides and/or angles of a triangle is the **computation of the triangle's area**. The <u>simplest formula</u> for the area is $A = \left(\dfrac{1}{2}\right)(b)(h)$, where A = area, b = any of the three sides, and h = the height drawn to the side b.

10 **Example:** *What is the area of the following triangle ABC?*

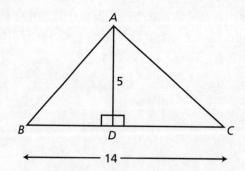

Solution: Since $b = 14$ and $h = 5$, the area is $\left(\dfrac{1}{2}\right)(14)(5) = 35$.

A <u>second formula</u> for the **area of a triangle** is based on **simply knowing the lengths of all the sides**. Suppose that a triangle has sides a, b, and c, and a **semiperimeter** of s.

By definition, $s = \left(\dfrac{1}{2}\right)(a+b+c)$.

Then the area (A) is given by the following formula: $A = \sqrt{(s)(s-a)(s-b)(s-c)}$.
This is called **Heron's formula**.

11 **Example:** *What is the area of $\triangle PRT$ from Example 8? (to the nearest hundredth)*

Solution:

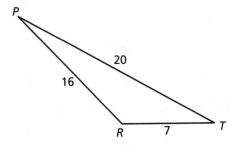

$s = \left(\dfrac{1}{2}\right)(16+7+20) = 21.5$.

Then $A = \sqrt{(21.5)(21.5-16)(21.5-7)(21.5-20)}$.

Simplifying, we get $A = \sqrt{(21.5)(5.5)(14.5)(1.5)} \approx \sqrt{2571.94} \approx 50.71$.

12 **Example:** *What is the area of $\triangle UVW$ from Example 9? (to the nearest hundredth)*

Solution:

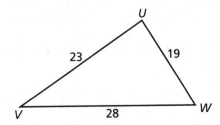

$s = \left(\dfrac{1}{2}\right)(23+28+19) = 35$.

Then $A = \sqrt{(35)(35-23)(35-28)(35-19)}$.

Simplifying, we get $A = \sqrt{(35)(12)(7)(16)} \approx \sqrt{47,040} \approx 216.89$.

A <u>third formula</u> for the area of a triangle is based on knowing the lengths of any two sides and the measure of the included angle. Let's redraw Figure 11.1.

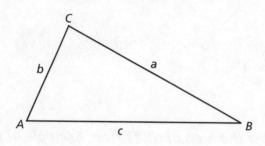

Figure 11.1

Suppose we know the values of a, c, and $\angle B$.
Then we have the lengths of two sides and the measure of the included angle.

The formula for the area (A) is given by $A = \left(\dfrac{1}{2}\right)(a)(c)(\sin \angle B)$. Likewise, if a, b, and $\angle C$ are known, then the area formula becomes $A = \left(\dfrac{1}{2}\right)(a)(b)(\sin \angle C)$.

13 **Example:** *What is the area of $\triangle DFH$ in Example 6? (to the nearest hundredth)*

Solution: Since $\angle H$ is the included angle between $\overline{DH}$ and $\overline{FH}$, we can use

the formula $A = \left(\dfrac{1}{2}\right)(25)(40)(\sin 33°) \approx (500)(0.5446) = 272.30$.

14 **Example:** *What is the area of $\triangle JLM$ in Example 7? (to the nearest hundredth)*

Solution: Since $\angle L$ is the included angle between $\overline{JL}$ and $\overline{LM}$, we can use

the formula $A = \left(\dfrac{1}{2}\right)(10)(34)(\sin 127°) \approx (170)(0.7986) \approx 135.76$.

MathFlash!

Even without a diagram, remember that an included angle must contain a common vertex of the sides that include it. For example, if $\overline{PQ}$ and $\overline{PR}$ are two sides of a triangle, the included angle must be $\angle P$. (The complete triangle is $\triangle PQR$, but you already knew that!)

Use the following diagram for 1, 2, and 3. Each problem is independent of the others.

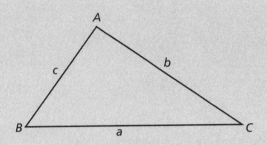

1. If *a* = 20, *c* = 17, and *m∠B* = 50°,
    what is the value of *b*?
    (to the nearest hundredth)   Answer: _____

2. If *a* = 24, *b* = 19, and *c* = 8,
    what is the measure of ∠C?
    (to the nearest degree)   Answer: _____

3. If *b* = 35, *c* = 40, and *m∠A* = 100°,
    what is the value of *a*?
    (to the nearest hundredth)   Answer: _____

4. In △*EKR*, *KR* = 15, *ER* = 25, and *EK* = 30,
    what is the measure of ∠*K*?
    (to the nearest degree)   Answer: _____

5. In △*BDF*, *DF* = 42, *BF* = 36, and *BD* = 18.
    What is the measure of ∠*F*?
    (to the nearest degree)   Answer: _____

6. In △*GHJ*, *GH* = 9, *HJ* = 16, and
    m∠H = 96°. What is the value of *GJ*?
    (to the nearest hundredth)   Answer: _____

Test Yourself! *(continued)*

7. What is the area of $\triangle ABC$, as described in question 1? (to the nearest hundredth)

    Answer: _____

8. What is the area of $\triangle EKR$, as described in question 4? (to the nearest hundredth)

    Answer: _____

9. What is the area of a triangle in which the lengths of the sides are 10, 17, and 22? (to the nearest hundredth)

    Answer: _____

10. In $\triangle QST$, $QS = 60$, $QT = 50$, and $m\angle Q = 38°$. What is the area of $\triangle QST$? (to the nearest hundredth)

    Answer: _____

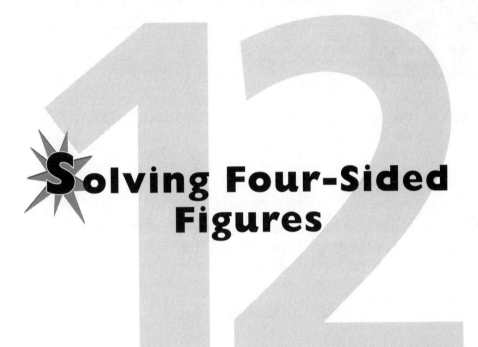

Solving Four-Sided Figures

In this lesson, we will explore the use of the **Laws of Sines** and **Cosines** in order to solve for any missing angle or side of a four-sided figure. By using a diagonal, four-sided figures are split into two triangles. Be sure that you understand the information required in order to use either the Law of Sines or the Law of Cosines.

Your Goal: When you have completed this lesson, you should be able to solve for any missing part of a four-sided figure, given sufficient information about the known parts.

Solving Four-Sided Figures

The easiest type of four-sided figure is the **square**. Consider Figure 12.1 shown below.

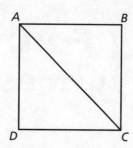

Figure 12.1

In square $ABCD$, with diagonal $\overline{AC}$, $m\angle DAB = m\angle B = m\angle BCD = m\angle D = 90°$. Since the diagonal $\overline{AC}$ bisects each of $\angle DAB$ and $\angle BCD$, we can determine that $m\angle DAC = m\angle CAB = m\angle BCA = m\angle ACD = 45°$.

All four sides of the square are equal in length, and the length of each diagonal equals the length of each side multiplied by $\sqrt{2}$.

1 **Example:** *In Figure 12.1, if AC = 10, what is the value of AB? (to the nearest hundredth)*

Solution: Since $AC = (AB)(\sqrt{2})$, $AB = \dfrac{AC}{\sqrt{2}} = \dfrac{10}{\sqrt{2}} \approx \dfrac{10}{1.414} \approx 7.07$.

The second type of four-sided figure to consider is the **rectangle**. Look at Figure 12.2 shown below.

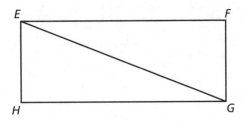

Figure 12.2

In rectangle *EFGH*, $m\angle HEF = m\angle F = m\angle FGH = m\angle H = 90°$. Opposite sides are equal, so that *EF* = *GH* and *EH* = *FG*. The diagonal $\overline{EG}$ does not bisect either of $\angle HEF$ or $\angle FGH$.

2 | **Example:** | *If EF = 17 and FG = 8, what is the value of EG? (to the nearest hundredth)*

Solution: Using the Pythagorean theorem, $(EG)^2 = 17^2 + 8^2 = 289 + 64 = 353$. Then $EG = \sqrt{353} \approx 18.79$.

3 | **Example:** | *Using the information in Example 1, what is the measure of $\angle GEF$? (to the nearest degree)*

Solution: Since $\triangle EFG$ is a right triangle, with a right angle at *F*, we can use the tangent ratio. Tan $\angle GEF = \dfrac{8}{17}$, so $\angle GEF = \tan^{-1}\left(\dfrac{8}{17}\right) \approx 25°$.

MathFlash!

Since you also knew that EG ≈ 18.79, you could have used either the sine ratio or the cosine ratio to determine the measure of $\angle GEF$. If you had selected the sine ratio, then $\angle GEF = \sin^{-1}\left(\dfrac{8}{18.79}\right) \approx 25°$.

4 **Example:** *In rectangle JKLM, JK = 23 and the diagonal JL = 27. What is the measure of ∠KJL? (to the nearest degree)*

Solution: Let's draw the picture.

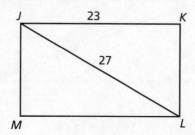

Since △*JKL* is a right triangle, we can use the cosine ratio.

Then $\cos \angle KLJ = \dfrac{23}{27}$. Thus, $\angle KLJ = \cos^{-1}\left(\dfrac{23}{27}\right) \approx 32°$.

5 **Example:** *Using the information in Example 4, what is the value of KL? (to the nearest hundredth)*

Solution: This one is wide open! We can use (a) the Pythagorean theorem, (b) the tangent ratio, or (c) the sine ratio.
If we use the Pythagorean theorem, then $23^2 + (KL)^2 = 27^2$.
So, $(KL)^2 = 27^2 - 23^2 = 200$.
Thus, $KL = \sqrt{200} \approx 14.14$.

The third type of four-sided figure we will consider is the **rhombus**. You recall that a rhombus appears as a "twisted" square. All four sides are congruent, but the angles at each vertex are not 90°. Figure 12.3 shows rhombus *NPQR*, with diagonal $\overline{NQ}$

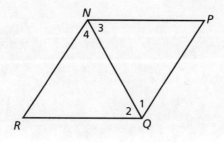

Figure 12.3

In a rhombus, each diagonal does bisect the angles whose vertices are the end points of the diagonal. Also, note that each of △*PNQ* and △*RNQ* are congruent isosceles triangles. Thus, $m\angle 1 = m\angle 2 = m\angle 3 = m\angle 4$. Also, $m\angle R = m\angle P$.

6 **Example:** *In Figure 12.3, if NP = 16 and m∠P = 52°, what is the value of NQ? (to the nearest hundredth)*

Solution: First note that $PQ = 16$, since all sides of a rhombus are congruent. Since we know two sides and an included angle in $\triangle NPQ$, we can use the Law of Cosines. $(NQ)^2 = 16^2 + 16^2 - (2)(16)(16)(\cos 52°)$. Simplifying, $(NQ)^2 = 256 + 256 - (512)(\cos 52°) \approx 196.78$. Finally, $NQ = \sqrt{196.78} \approx 14.03$.

MathFlash!

In Example 6, we could have used the Law of Sines, if we had calculated the measure of ∠1 (or ∠3). With just a touch of algebra and remembering that m∠1 + m∠3 + m∠P = 180°, we find that m∠1 = 64°. Using the Law of Sines, $\dfrac{16}{\sin 64°} = \dfrac{NQ}{\sin 52°}$.
So (NQ)(sin 64°) = (16)(sin 52°). You should get NQ ≈ 14.03.

7 **Example:** *Given rhombus STUV with TV representing the longer of the two diagonals, if TU = 24 and TV = 39, what is the measure of ∠VTU? (to the nearest degree)*

Solution: Here is a drawing:

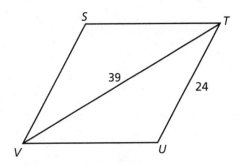

Since $TU = UV$, we know that $UV = 24$.
Now we have the lengths of all three sides of $\triangle VTU$.
So, we use the Law of Cosines:
$(UV)^2 = (TU)^2 + (TV)^2 - (2)(TU)(TV)(\cos \angle VTU)$.
By substitution, $24^2 = 24^2 + 39^2 - (2)(24)(39)(\cos \angle VTU)$.
Simplifying, we get $576 = 576 + 1521 - (1872)(\cos \angle VTU)$.
Then $-1521 = -(1872)(\cos \angle VTU)$.

Since $\cos \angle VTU = \dfrac{1521}{1872}$, $\angle VTU = \cos^{-1}\left(\dfrac{1521}{1872}\right) \approx 36°$.

8 **Example:**   *Using the information from Example 7, what is the measure of ∠U? (to the nearest degree)*

Solution: If you are in a rush, this solution is real quick!
$m\angle TVU = m\angle VTU = 36°$.
Thus, $m\angle U = 180° - 36° - 36° = 108°$.

MathFlash!

If you do use the Law of Sines, the correct proportion will be $\dfrac{39}{\sin \angle U} = \dfrac{24}{\sin 36°}$. However, you need to be careful! Because $\overline{TV}$ is the <u>longer</u> diagonal, you must use the <u>second</u> quadrant angle when you take the inverse sine in your last step. You should still get the answer of 108°.

The fourth (and last) type of four-sided figure we will discuss is the **parallelogram.** A parallelogram appears as a "twisted" rectangle. Figure 12.4 shows parallelogram *WXYZ*, with shorter diagonal $\overline{WY}$.

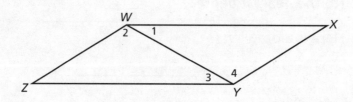

Figure 12.4

Each pair of opposite sides is parallel and congruent. As with a rectangle, each diagonal does not bisect either of the angles whose vertices are the end points of the diagonal. Thus, $m\angle 1 \neq m\angle 2$ and $m\angle 3 \neq m\angle 4$. However, you may recall from your study of geometry that alternate interior angles of parallel lines are congruent. This means that $m\angle 1 = m\angle 3$ and $m\angle 2 = m\angle 4$.

9 **Example:** *Using Figure 12.4, if m ∠1 = 25°, WX = 13, and XY = 9, what is the measure of ∠4? (to the nearest degree). Remember to assume that WY is the shorter diagonal.*

Solution: Since we are given two sides and a non-included angle of $\triangle WXY$, our best bet is to use the Law of Sines. So, $\dfrac{WX}{\sin \angle 4} = \dfrac{XY}{\sin \angle 1}$.

Then by substitution, $\dfrac{13}{\sin \angle 4} = \dfrac{9}{\sin 25°}$.

Using 0.4226 for the value of sin 25° and cross-multiplying, we get $(9)(\sin \angle 4) = (13)(0.4226) \approx 5.4938$.

This leads to $\sin \angle 4 = \dfrac{5.4938}{9}$.

Finally, $\angle 4 = \sin^{-1}\left(\dfrac{5.4938}{9}\right) \approx 142°$.

MathFlash!

Hopefully, you remembered to use the second quadrant answer of 142° and not the first quadrant answer of 38° when you found the inverse sine value. Luckily, there is a "safety net" check! If you did use the answer of 38°, then m∠X = 180° – 25° – 38° = 117°. This cannot be correct because ∠X is opposite the shorter diagonal, and therefore has to be an acute angle. (This type of check is also valid for the rhombus.)

10 **Example:** *Using the information in Example 9, use the Law of Cosines to determine the value of WY? (to the nearest hundredth)*

Solution: Let's first find the measure of ∠X. m∠X = 180° – 25° – 142° = 13°.
By the Law of Cosines, $(WY)^2 = (WX)^2 + (XY)^2 - (2)(WX)(XY)(\cos \angle X)$.
By substitution, $(WY)^2 = 13^2 + 9^2 - (2)(13)(9)(\cos 13°)$.
Using 0.9744 for the value of cos 13°,
$(WY)^2 \approx 169 + 81 - 228.0096 = 21.9904$.

Finally, $WY = \sqrt{21.9904} \approx 4.69$.

11   **Example:**   *In parallelogram ABCD, let CD represent one of the bases. If AB = 27, BC = 16, and m∠B = 118°, what is the measure of ∠DAC? (to the nearest degree).*

Solution: Our best approach begins with an appropriate diagram:

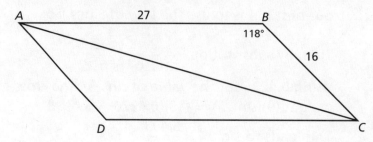

The information we are given pertains to △BAC, but we need to find the value of an angle in △DAC. There is no need to panic because $m\angle DAC = m\angle ACB$, (alternate interior angles of parallel lines).

Since we are given the values of two sides and an included angle, we can use the Law of Cosines to first find the value of AC in △ABC. Then $(AC)^2 = 27^2 + 16^2 - (2)(27)(16)(\cos 118°)$.
Using −0.4695 as the value of cos 118°,
$(AC)^2 \approx 729 + 256 - (-405.65) = 1390.65$. So, $AC \approx 37.29$.

Now we can use either the Law of Cosines or the Law of Sines to find the measure of ∠ACB, which is equivalent to the measure of ∠DAC.

Let's use the Law of Sines, so that $\dfrac{27}{\sin \angle ACB} = \dfrac{37.29}{\sin 118°}$.
Using 0.8829 as the value of sin 118°, we get
$(37.29)(\sin \angle ACB) = (27)(0.8829) \approx 23.83$.

Finally, since $\sin \angle ACB = \dfrac{23.83}{37.29}$, $\angle ACB = \sin^{-1}\left(\dfrac{23.83}{37.29}\right) \approx 40°$.
Thus, $\angle DAC = \angle ACB = 40°$.

Unfortunately, this solution could not be shortened. Whenever we are given the values of two sides of a triangle and the value of the included angle, we must resort to first using the Law of Cosines. This procedure will yield the value of the missing side.

If the question involves solving for a missing angle value, we can then use either the Law of Sines or the Law of Cosines. Notice that we were careful to select the first quadrant value when finding the inverse sine of $\dfrac{23.83}{37.29}$.

If you had mistakenly chosen 140° as your final answer for the measure of ∠ACB, the error would have been a glaring one. You would have had two obtuse angles in △ACB!

12 Example: *Using the information in Example 11, what is the measure of ∠ACD?*

Solution: We will use the most painless approach possible. You know from geometry that consecutive angles of a parallelogram are supplementary.
This implies that $m\angle B + m\angle BCD = 180°$.
Since $m\angle B = 118°$, then $m\angle BCD = 62°$.
But $m\angle BCD = m\angle ACB + m\angle ACD$.
By substitution, $62° = 40° + m\angle ACD$. Thus, $m\angle ACD = 22°$.

Test Yourself!

1.   In square *EFGH*, *EF* = 15. To the nearest hundredth, what is the value of *EG*?

Answer: _____

2.   In rectangle *JKLM*, *KM* = 20 and *KL* = 11. To the nearest hundredth, what is the value of *LM*?

Answer: _____

3.   Using the information in question 2, what is the measure of ∠*KML*?

Answer: _____

4.   Consider the following rectangle:

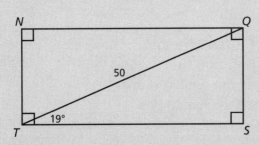

What is the value of *QS* + *ST*?
(to the nearest hundredth)

Answer: _____

Test Yourself! *(continued)*

5. Consider the following rhombus:

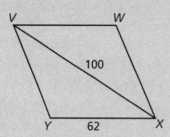

What is the measure of ∠*VXY*?
(to the nearest degree)   *Answer:* _____

6. Using the information in question 5,
    what is the measure of ∠*Y*?   *Answer:* _____

7. In rhombus *ZBDF*, in which the
    measure of ∠*Z* is 52° and *ZB* = 48,
    what is the value of *BF*?
    (to the nearest hundredth)   *Answer:* _____

8. Consider the following parallelogram:

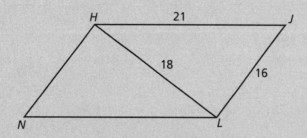

What is the measure of ∠*JLN*? (to the
nearest degree) (<u>Hint</u>: First find the
measure of ∠*J*, then use the well-known
theorem concerning consecutive angles
of a parallelogram.)   *Answer:* _____

Test Yourself! *(continued)*

9.   Consider the following parallelogram:

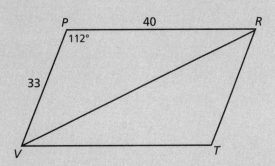

To the nearest hundredth, what is
the value of *RV*?   *Answer:* _____

10. In parallelogram *WXYZ*, *WX* = 20,
XZ = 14, and *m∠W* = 36°. What is
the measure of ∠*WXZ*? (to the
nearest degree)   *Answer:* _____

QUIZ THREE

Use the following triangle for questions 1 and 2. (Each question is independent of the other.)

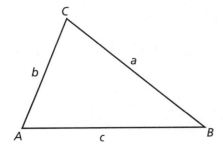

1. If c =15, $m\angle C$ = 80°, and $m\angle B$ = 42°, what is the value of b? (to the nearest hundredth)

   A   7.88

   B   9.03

   C   10.19

   D   11.34

2. If $m\angle A$ = 65°, a = 45, and b = 26, what is the measure of $\angle B$? (to the nearest degree)

   A   41°

   B   38°

   C   35°

   D   32°

3. In rectangle WXYZ, WX is one of the lengths and XY is one of the widths. If WY = 25 and $m\angle ZWY$ = 72°, what is the value of WZ + ZY? (to the nearest hundredth)

   A   27.40

   B   29.45

   C   31.50

   D   33.55

Use the following triangle for questions 4 and 5. (Each question is independent of the other.)

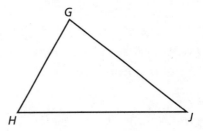

4. If GH = 18, HJ = 27 and $m\angle H$ = 74°, what is the value of GJ? (to the nearest hundredth)

   A   25.59

   B   28.02

   C   30.45

   D   32.88

5. If GH = 6, GJ = 24, and $m\angle G$ = 100°, what is the measure of $\angle J$? (to the nearest degree)

   A   25°

   B   19°

   C   13°

   D   7°

6. Consider the following rhombus:

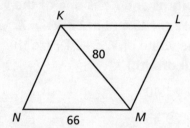

What is the measure of ∠*KMN*? (to the nearest degree)

A 50°

B 53°

C 56°

D 59°

7. In △*PQR*, *QR* = 52, *m∠R* = 105°, and *m∠Q* = 29°. What is the value of *PQ*? (to the nearest hundredth)

A 59.27

B 62.79

C 66.31

D 69.83

8. Consider the following parallelogram:

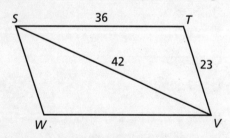

What is the measure of ∠*WVT*? (to the nearest degree)

A 100°

B 96°

C 92°

D 88°

9. In parallelogram *BDFH*, *BH* = 33, *m∠B* = 140°, and *m∠BHD* = 24°. What is the value of *DH*? (to the nearest hundredth)

A 76.96

B 68.69

C 60.42

D 52.15

10. What is the area of a triangle with sides of 8, 11, and 15? (to the nearest hundredth)

A 42.85

B 46.15

C 49.45

D 52.75

Solving Trigonometric Equations—Part I

In this lesson, we will explore the techniques that are used to **solve** some **trigonometric equations**. Each equation will contain only one trigonometric ratio. Before you begin this lesson, be sure that you recall how to solve both linear and quadratic equations in one variable.

Your Goal: When you have completed this lesson, you should be able to solve for the value(s) of an unknown angle in equations that contain only one trigonometric ratio.

Throughout this lesson, we will seek angle values, to the nearest degree, that lie between 0° and 360°, inclusive. The Greek letter θ (pronounced "thay'-tuh") will be used to represent the angle.

LESSON 13

Solving Trigonometric Equations—Part 1

1 **Example:** *What is (are) the value(s) of θ in the equation sin θ + 16.5 = 17.3?*

Solution: This is a linear equation in which sin θ represents the unknown variable. By subtracting 16.5 from each side of the equation, we get sin θ = 0.8. Then θ = $\sin^{-1}$(0.8) ≈ 53° or 127°.

MathFlash!

You must remember to check each quadrant when finding the value of any inverse trigonometric ratio. In this case, the sine ratio is positive in both the first and second quadrants.

II	I
III	IV

2 **Example:** *What is (are) the value(s) of θ in the equation 3 tan θ – 0.56 = 1.25?*

Solution: First add 0.56 to each side of the equation to get 3 tan θ = 1.81.
By dividing each side by 3, we get tan θ ≈ 0.6033.
Then θ ≈ $\tan^{-1}$(0.6033) ≈ 31° or 211°.

3 **Example:** *What is (are) the value(s) of θ in the equation 4 sec θ + 3 = 2 sec θ – 4?*

Solution: Can you see why this equation is very similar to the algebraic equation 4x + 3 = 2x – 4?
First subtract 2 sec θ from each side to get 2 sec θ + 3 = –4.
By subtracting 3 from each side, we get 2 sec θ = –7.

So $\sec θ = -\frac{7}{2}$, which means that $θ = \sec^{-1}\left(-\frac{7}{2}\right) ≈ 107°$ or 253°.

4 **Example:** *What is (are) the value(s) of θ in the equation 6(csc θ − 2) = 13 csc θ ?*

Solution: Similar to the technique you have used in algebra, we use the Distributive Property to remove the parentheses.
This equation becomes 6 csc θ − 12 = 13 csc θ .
Subtract 6 csc θ from each side to get −12 = 7 csc θ.

Then $\theta \approx \csc^{-1}\left(-\dfrac{12}{7}\right)$, which means that θ ≈ 216° or 324°.

5 **Example:** *What is (are) the value(s) of θ in the equation cos² θ − 0.6 = 0.3?*

Solution: This is a quadratic equation in which cos θ represents the unknown variable. The notation cos² θ <u>always</u> means the same as (cos θ)².
It does <u>not</u> mean cos(θ ²).
Add 0.6 to each side to get cos² θ = 0.9.
Taking the square root of each side leads to cos θ ≈ ±0.9487.
This means that θ = cos⁻¹(0.9487) or θ = cos⁻¹(−0.9487).

Each of these last two equations has two answers, so we will get four values of θ.
When θ = cos⁻¹(0.9487), θ ≈ 18° or 342°.
Also, when θ = cos⁻¹(−0.9487), θ ≈ 162° or 198°.

MathFlash!

In any algebraic equation in which x^2 equals a positive number, the values of x are the positive and negative values of the square root of that number. Thus, if $x^2 = 12$, then $x \pm \sqrt{12}$.

However, if you are faced with an equation such as $x^2 = -10$, then there is <u>no</u> real number solution. This means that a reduced equation such as sin² θ = −0.7 has <u>no</u> solution.

6 **Example:**   *What is (are) the value(s) of θ in the equation*
5 cot² θ − 0.75 = 2 cot² θ − 0.5?

Solution: This equation is similar to the one shown in Example 3.
First subtract 2 cot² θ from each side to get 3 cot² θ − 0.75 = − 0.5.
Next, add 0.75 to each side to get 3 cot² θ = 0.25.

Then cot² θ ≈ 0.0833, so cot θ = ±√0.0833 ≈ ±0.2887 .
When θ = cot⁻¹(0.2887), θ ≈ 74° or 254°.
When θ = cot⁻¹(−0.2887), θ ≈ 106° or 286°.

Before we embark on the last six practice examples, we will briefly **review three factoring techniques** from algebra.

One type is called **Common Term factoring**, for which we show three examples:

(a) $x^2 + 5x = (x)(x + 5)$

(b) $4y^2 - 6y = (2y)(2y - 3)$

(c) $5z^2 + 20z = (5z)(z + 4)$

In each of these three examples, the greatest common factor is placed into the first set of parentheses. Then this factor is divided into each term.

For example, in (b), $2y$ is the greatest common factor of each of $4y^2$ and $6y$. Thus, the first set of parentheses contains $2y$ and the second set of parentheses is found by dividing each of $4y^2$ and $6y$ by $2y$.

A second type of factoring is called **Difference of Two Squares**, for which we show three examples:

(a) $x^2 - 25 = (x - 5)(x + 5)$

(b) $9y^2 - 49 = (3y - 7)(3y + 7)$

(c) $-16z^2 + 1 = 1 - 16z^2 = (1 - 4z)(1 + 4z)$

In all of these examples, each of the two terms is a perfect square, separated by a minus sign. The two sets of parentheses are constructed by taking the square root of each term. In one set of parentheses, insert a minus sign between terms. In the other set of parentheses, insert a plus sign between terms.

For example, in (a), $(x)(x) = x^2$ and $(5)(5) = 25$.
Each set of parentheses will contain x and 5.
Notice that one set of parentheses has a minus sign between terms, whereas the other set of parentheses has a plus sign.
(It does not matter if the set of parentheses with the plus sign appears first.)

A third type of factoring is called **Trial and Error Factoring**, for which we show six examples:

(a) $x^2 + 7x + 12 = (x + 4)(x + 3)$

(b) $x^2 + 5x - 36 = (x - 4)(x + 9)$

(c) $y^2 - 16y + 64 = (y - 8)(y - 8)$, which can also be written as $(y - 8)^2$

(d) $2y^2 - 5y - 3 = (2y + 1)(y - 3)$

(e) $7z^2 + 18z + 8 = (7z + 4)(z + 2)$

(f) $15z^2 + z - 6 = (5z - 3)(3z + 2)$.

In each of these examples, the trinomial (3-term expression) is factored as two binomials (2-term expressions). This technique is often called "Trial and Error" factoring because there is an element of guessing.

Looking at (f), $15z^2$ can be obtained by $(5z)(3z)$ or by $(15z)(1z)$.
Likewise, the number 6 can be found as a product with either (3)(2) or with (1)(6).

It is suggested that you carefully review these major categories of factoring before looking at the next six examples that deal with trigonometric ratios.

---

7 **Example:** *What is (are) the value(s) of θ in the equation tan² θ + 2 tan θ – 3 = 0?*

Solution: If we treat $\tan \theta$ as if it were an x, then this equation becomes $x^2 + 2x - 3 = 0$.
Since $x^2 + 2x - 3$ can be factored as $(x + 3)(x - 1)$, the original equation can be written as $(\tan \theta + 3)(\tan \theta - 1) = 0$.
When a product equals zero, we set each factor of that product equal to zero and solve.
So, we solve $\tan \theta + 3 = 0$ and $\tan \theta - 1 = 0$.
For the first of these two equations, $\theta = \tan^{-1}(-3) \approx 108°$ or $288°$.
For the equation $\tan \theta - 1 = 0$, $\theta = \tan^{-1}(1) = 45°$ or $225°$.

8 Example: *What is (are) the value(s) of θ in the equation 9 sin² θ – 4 = 0?*

Solution: We will consider this equation as a difference of two squares.
$9 \sin^2 \theta - 4$ can be factored as $(3 \sin \theta - 2)(3 \sin \theta + 2)$.
This means that $(3 \sin \theta - 2)(3 \sin \theta + 2) = 0$.

If $3 \sin \theta - 2 = 0$, then $\sin \theta = \dfrac{2}{3}$.

This leads to $\theta = \sin^{-1}\left(\dfrac{2}{3}\right) \approx 42°$ or $138°$.

If $3 \sin \theta + 2 = 0$, then $\sin \theta = -\dfrac{2}{3}$.

This leads to $\theta = \sin^{-1}\left(-\dfrac{2}{3}\right) \approx 222°$ or $318°$.

MathFlash!

At first glance, it appears that each of these quadratic equations that can be factored will contain four answers. However, this is not always true. Although the tangent and cotangent ratios can assume all values, there are restrictions on the other four trigonometric ratios. Here is a summary of their restrictions, without a formal proof.
For any angle θ:

- $-1 \le \sin \theta \le 1$
- $-1 \le \cos \theta \le 1$
- $\sec \theta \ge 1$ or $\sec \theta \le -1$
- and $\csc \theta \ge 1$ or $\csc \theta \le -1$

9 Example: *What is (are) the value(s) of θ in the equation 2 cos² θ – 5 cos θ = 0?*

Solution: Think of this equation as $2x^2 - 5x = 0$, which could be written in factored form as $(x)(2x - 5) = 0$.
Replacing x with $\cos \theta$, we can write $\cos \theta = 0$ or $2 \cos \theta - 5 = 0$.
If $\cos \theta = 0$, then $\theta = \cos^{-1}(0) = 90°$ or $270°$.

If $2 \cos \theta - 5 = 0$, then $\theta = \cos^{-1}\left(\dfrac{5}{2}\right)$, which does not exist.

Thus, the only two answers are $90°$ and $270°$.

10 Example: **What is (are) the value(s) of θ in the equation −1 + 36 cot² θ = 0?**

Solution: Rewrite the equation as 36 cot² θ − 1 = 0.
We recognize the expression on the left side as the difference of two squares.
So we can write the equation as (6 cot θ − 1)(6 cot θ + 1) = 0.

If 6 cot θ − 1 = 0, then $\theta = \cot^{-1}\left(\dfrac{1}{6}\right) \approx 81°$ or 261°.

If 6 cot θ + 1 = 0, then $\theta = \cot^{-1}\left(-\dfrac{1}{6}\right) \approx 99°$ or 279°.

11 Example: **What is (are) the value(s) of θ in the equation
4 csc² θ − 11 csc θ + 6 = 0?**

Solution: If you are in a big hurry, then this is definitely not the problem you would want to solve!
With some patience, you should be able to rewrite this equation in factored form as (4 csc θ − 3)(csc θ − 2) = 0.

If 4 csc θ − 3 = 0, then $\theta = \csc^{-1}\left(\dfrac{3}{4}\right)$, which does not exist.

But if csc θ − 2 = 0, then θ = csc⁻¹(2) = 30° or 150°.

12 Example: **What is (are) the value(s) of θ in the equation
3 sec² θ + 2 sec θ − 5 = 0?**

Solution: This is another example of Trial and Error factoring.
In factored form, this equation can be written as
(3 sec θ + 5)(sec θ − 1) = 0.

If 3 sec θ + 5 = 0, then $\theta = \sec^{-1}\left(-\dfrac{5}{3}\right) = 127°$ or 233°.

If sec θ − 1 = 0, then θ = sec⁻¹(1) = 0°.

Notice that this example has exactly *three* answers.

MathFlash!

The maximum number of answers for quadratic equations with trigonometric ratios is <u>four</u>. However, it is possible to have any number of solutions less than four, including no solution.

One example of an equation with no solution is $\cos^2 \theta + \cos \theta - 6 = 0$. Using factoring, this equation can be written as $(\cos \theta + 3)(\cos \theta - 2) = 0$.
If $\cos \theta + 3 = 0$, then $\theta = \cos^{-1}(-3)$, which does not exist.
Also, if $\cos \theta - 2 = 0$, then $\theta = \cos^{-1}(2)$, which does not exist.

Thus, there is no possible value of θ that satisfies the original equation.

 Test Yourself!

For each problem, determine the value(s) of θ for which the equation is true. Each equation has at least one solution.

1. $4 \cos \theta + 5 = 8$ *Answer(s):* _____

2. $\cot \theta + 0.15 = -2.6$ *Answer(s):* _____

3. $8(\sin \theta - 1) = 17 \sin \theta$ *Answer(s):* _____

4. $4 \csc^2 \theta + 2.3 = 9.5$ *Answer(s):* _____

5. $9 \tan \theta - 3 = 4 \tan \theta - 17$ *Answer(s):* _____

6. $16 \sec^2 \theta - 49 = 0$ *Answer(s):* _____

7. $3 \tan^2 \theta - \tan \theta = 0$ *Answer(s):* _____

8. $7 \sin^2 \theta - 2 \sin \theta - 5 = 0$ *Answer(s):* _____

9. $\cot^2 \theta - 8 \cot \theta + 12 = 0$ *Answer(s):* _____

10. $5 \cos^2 \theta + 17 \cos \theta + 6 = 0$ *Answer(s):* _____

Solving Trigonometric Equations—Part 2

In this lesson, we will explore the techniques that are used to solve equations that contain **two different trigonometric ratios**. In order to solve these equations, we will need to use a trigonometric identity that allows us to rewrite the equation (a) with only a single trigonometric ratio or (b) with two trigonometric ratios, one of which will represent a common factor.

Your Goal: When you have completed this lesson, you should be able to solve for the value(s) of an unknown angle in equations that contain two trigonometric ratios.

As in Lesson 13, we will seek angle values, to the nearest degree, that lie between 0° and 360°, inclusive. The Greek letter θ will be used to represent the unknown angle in each example.

Solving Trigonometric Equations—Part 2

You have been using three basic trigonometric identities:

$$\csc \theta = \frac{1}{\sin \theta}, \; \sec \theta = \frac{1}{\cos \theta}, \; \text{and} \; \cot \theta = \frac{1}{\tan \theta}.$$

Let's review two more common identities, namely, $\tan \theta = \dfrac{\sin \theta}{\cos \theta}$ and $\cot \theta = \dfrac{\cos \theta}{\sin \theta}$.

We have shown why $\tan \theta = \dfrac{\sin \theta}{\cos \theta}$ must always be true. With a right triangle as our model, we defined sin θ as the ratio $\dfrac{\text{opposite side}}{\text{hypotenuse}}$ and cos θ as the ratio $\dfrac{\text{adjacent side}}{\text{hypotenuse}}$. Then by substitution, $\dfrac{\sin \theta}{\cos \theta} = \dfrac{\text{opposite side}}{\text{hypotenuse}} \div \dfrac{\text{adjacent side}}{\text{hypotenuse}} = \dfrac{\text{opposite side}}{\text{hypotenuse}} \times \dfrac{\text{hypotenuse}}{\text{adjacent side}} = \dfrac{\text{opposite side}}{\text{adjacent side}} = \tan \theta$.

Note that "hypotenuse" has been canceled from the numerator of one fraction and the denominator of a second fraction.

Also, it follows that $\cot \theta = \dfrac{1}{\tan \theta} = 1 \div \dfrac{\sin \theta}{\cos \theta} = \dfrac{\cos \theta}{\sin \theta}$.

1 **Example:** *What is (are) the value(s) of θ in the equation 4 cos θ – sec θ = 0?*

Solution: Let's replace sec θ with $\dfrac{1}{\cos \theta}$, so that the equation becomes $4 \cos \theta - \dfrac{1}{\cos \theta} = 0$.

Multiplying by cos θ, we get 4 cos² θ – 1 = 0.

Factoring the left side leads to (2 cos θ – 1)(2 cos θ + 1) = 0.

If 2 cos θ – 1 = 0, then $\theta = \cos^{-1}\left(\dfrac{1}{2}\right) = 60°$ or 300°.

If 2 cos θ + 1 = 0, then $\theta = \cos^{-1}\left(-\dfrac{1}{2}\right) = 120°$ or 240°.

Thus, the four answers are 60°, 120°, 240°, or 300°.

MathFlash!

Always remember to check that when you multiply an equation by any quantity in a denominator, that quantity is not equal to zero.

So, if $\cos \theta$ had a value of zero in Example 1, the fraction $\dfrac{1}{\cos \theta}$ would have been undefined.

2 **Example:** *What is (are) the value(s) of θ in the equation $\sin \theta - 2 \tan \theta = 0$?*

Solution: By using the identity $\tan \theta = \dfrac{\sin \theta}{\cos \theta}$, we can rewrite this equation

as $\sin \theta - \dfrac{2 \sin \theta}{\cos \theta} = 0$.

Multiplying by $\cos \theta$, we get $\sin \theta \cos \theta - 2 \sin \theta = 0$.

Then $(\sin \theta)(\cos \theta - 2) = 0$. If $\sin \theta = 0$, then $\theta = \sin^{-1}(0) = 0°$ or $180°$.

If $\cos \theta - 2 = 0$, then $\theta = \cos^{-1}(2)$, which is not possible.

Thus, the only answers are $0°$ or $180°$.

3 **Example:** *What is (are) the value(s) of θ in the equation $\cot \theta - \dfrac{\tan \theta}{5} = 0$?*

Solution: Replace $\cot \theta$ with $\dfrac{1}{\tan \theta}$. The equation becomes $\dfrac{1}{\tan \theta} - \dfrac{\tan \theta}{5} = 0$.

Next multiply this equation by $5 \tan \theta$ to get $5 - \tan^2 \theta = 0$.

Now, since $\tan^2 \theta = 5$, this implies that $\tan \theta = \sqrt{5}$ or $\tan \theta = -\sqrt{5}$.

For the first of these two conditions, $\theta = \tan^{-1}(\sqrt{5}) \approx 66°$ or $246°$.

Also, if $\tan \theta = -\sqrt{5}$, then $\theta = \tan^{-1}(-\sqrt{5}) \approx 114°$ or 294.

4 **Example:** *What is (are) the value(s) of θ in the equation $6 \cos \theta + 4 \cot \theta = 0$?*

Solution: Use the identity $\cot \theta = \dfrac{\cos \theta}{\sin \theta}$, to rewrite the equation as

$6 \cos \theta + \dfrac{4 \cos \theta}{\sin \theta} = 0$.

Multiply by $\sin \theta$, to get $6 \cos \theta \sin \theta + 4 \cos \theta = 0$.

Factor out the common term $2 \cos \theta$ to get $(2 \cos \theta)(3 \sin \theta + 2) = 0$.

If $2 \cos \theta = 0$, then $\theta = \cos^{-1}(0) = 90°$ or $270°$.

If $3 \sin \theta + 2 = 0$, then $\theta = \sin^{-1}\left(-\dfrac{2}{3}\right) \approx 222°$ or $318°$.

We will now add three more popular trigonometric identities to our growing list:

(a) $\sin^2 \theta + \cos^2 \theta = 1$,

(b) $\tan^2 \theta + 1 = \sec^2 \theta$, and

(c) $\cot^2 \theta + 1 = \csc^2 \theta$.

These three identities are often referred to as **Trigonometric Pythagorean Identities.** Before we show the derivation of each one, recall that for any acute angle of a right triangle, (opposite side)² + (adjacent side)² = (hypotenuse)². This is a direct application of the Pythagorean theorem.

We will demonstrate each of these three statements by using the basic definitions of these trigonometric ratios.

(a) $\sin^2 \theta + \cos^2 \theta = \dfrac{(\text{opposite side})^2}{(\text{hypotenuse})^2} + \dfrac{(\text{adjacent side})^2}{(\text{hypotenuse})^2} =$

$$\dfrac{(\text{opposite side})^2 + (\text{adjacent side})^2}{(\text{hypotenuse})^2} = \dfrac{(\text{hypotenuse})^2}{(\text{hypotenuse})^2} = 1$$

For parts (b) and (c), we will use p to represent the opposite side, a to represent the adjacent side, and h to represent the hypotenuse. With these abbreviations, $p^2 + a^2 = h^2$,

(b) $\tan^2 \theta + 1 = \dfrac{p^2}{a^2} + 1 = \dfrac{p^2}{a^2} + \dfrac{a^2}{a^2} + \dfrac{p^2 + a^2}{a^2} = \dfrac{h^2}{a^2}$.

Since $\dfrac{h}{a}$ represents the secant ratio, $\dfrac{h^2}{a^2}$ is equivalent to $\sec^2 \theta$.

(c) $\cot^2 \theta + 1 = \dfrac{a^2}{p^2} + 1 = \dfrac{a^2}{p^2} + \dfrac{p^2}{p^2} + \dfrac{a^2 + p^2}{p^2} = \dfrac{h^2}{p^2}$.

Since $\dfrac{h}{p}$ represents the cosecant ratio, $\dfrac{h^2}{p^2}$ is equivalent to $\csc^2 \theta$.

5 **Example:**   *What is (are) the value(s) of θ in the equation*

$\sin^2 \theta + \cos^2 \theta + 8 \cos \theta = 0$?

Solution: Since $\sin^2 \theta + \cos^2 \theta = 1$, the equation can be written as $1 + 8 \cos \theta = 0$. After subtracting 1 and then dividing 8, we get $\cos \theta = -\dfrac{1}{8}$.

So, $\theta = \cos^{-1}\left(-\dfrac{1}{8}\right) \approx 97°$ or $263°$.

6 **Example:** *What is (are) the value(s) of θ in the equation*
$5 \sin^2 θ - 6 \sin θ + 5 \cos^2 θ = 0$?

Solution: The most important advice to be heeded is not to panic.
Let's rewrite the equation as $5 \sin^2 θ + 5 \cos^2 θ - 6 \sin θ = 0$.
We know that $\sin^2 θ + \cos^2 θ = 1$.
So $5 \sin^2 θ + 5 \cos^2 θ$, which is $(5)(\sin^2 θ + \cos^2 θ)$, must be $(5)(1) = 5$.
Now the equation simplifies to $5 - 6 \sin θ = 0$.
This is much better!

The next steps are $-6 \sin θ = -5$, followed by $θ = \sin^{-1}\left(\dfrac{5}{6}\right) \approx 56°$ or $124°$.

7 **Example:** *What is (are) the value(s) of θ in the equation*
$3 \sec θ + \tan^2 θ + 1 = 0$?

Solution: Since $\tan^2 θ + 1 = \sec^2 θ$, the original equation can be written
as $3 \sec θ + \sec^2 θ = 0$.
Factor the left side to get $(\sec θ)(3 + \sec θ) = 0$.
If $\sec θ = 0$, then $θ = \sec^{-1}(0)$, which is impossible.
If $3 + \sec θ = 0$, then $θ = \sec^{-1}(-3) \approx 109°$ or $251°$.

8 **Example:** *What is (are) the value(s) of θ in the equation*
$4 \tan^2 θ - 4 \sec θ + 1 = 0$?

Solution: Since $\tan^2 θ + 1 = \sec^2 θ$, it is also true that $\tan^2 θ = \sec^2 θ - 1$.
Now rewrite the original equation as $4(\sec^2 θ - 1) - 4 \sec θ + 1 = 0$.
Remove parentheses and combine similar terms to get
$4 \sec^2 θ - 4 \sec θ - 3 = 0$.
At this point, you can anticipate the use of factoring to solve for θ.
Using Trial and Error factoring, we get $(2 \sec θ + 1)(2 \sec θ - 3) = 0$.

If $2 \sec θ + 1 = 0$, then $θ = \sec^{-1}\left(-\dfrac{1}{2}\right)$, which is impossible.

If $2 \sec θ - 3 = 0$, then $θ = \sec^{-1}\left(\dfrac{3}{2}\right) \approx 48°$ or $312°$.

9 **Example:** *What is (are) the value(s) of θ in the equation*
$$\cot^2 \theta - 3 \csc \theta - 3 = 0?$$

Solution: Since $\cot^2 \theta + 1 = \csc^2 \theta$, we can replace $\cot^2 \theta$ with $\csc^2 \theta - 1$.
The equation will read as $(\csc^2 \theta - 1) - 3 \csc \theta - 3 = 0$.
Remove the parentheses and combine similar terms to get
$\csc^2 \theta - 3 \csc \theta - 4 = 0$.
Now factor the left side to get $(\csc \theta - 4)(\csc \theta + 1) = 0$.
If $\csc \theta - 4 = 0$, then $\theta = \csc^{-1}(4) \approx 14°$ or $166°$.
If $\csc \theta + 1 = 0$, then $\theta = \csc^{-1}(-1) = 270°$.

10 **Example:** *What is (are) the value(s) of θ in the equation*
$$2 \csc^2 \theta - \cot \theta - 17 = 0?$$

Solution: Rewrite the equation as $2(\cot^2 \theta + 1) - \cot \theta - 17 = 0$.
Remove the parentheses and combine similar terms to get
$2 \cot^2 \theta - \cot \theta - 15 = 0$.
Using Trial and Error factoring, this equation becomes
$(2 \cot \theta + 5)(\cot \theta - 3) = 0$.

If $2 \cot \theta + 5 = 0$, then $\theta = \cot^{-1}\left(-\dfrac{5}{2}\right) \approx 158°$ or $338°$.

If $\cot \theta - 3 = 0$, then $\theta = \cot^{-1}(3) \approx 18°$ or $198°$.

 Test Yourself!

For each problem, determine the value(s) of θ for which the equation is
true. Each equation has at least one solution.

1. $4 \sin \theta + \tan \theta = 0$ *Answer(s):* _____

2. $25 \sin \theta - 9 \csc \theta = 0$ *Answer(s):* _____

3. $3 \cos \theta - 7 \cot \theta = 0$ *Answer(s):* _____

4. $2 \tan \theta - \dfrac{\cot \theta}{4} = 0$ *Answer(s):* _____

5. $\sin^2 \theta - 5 \sin \theta + \cos^2 \theta = 0$ *Answer(s):* _____

6. $4 \sin^2 \theta + 4 \cos^2 \theta + 9 \cos \theta = 0$ *Answer(s):* _____

7. $\cot^2 \theta + 6 \csc \theta + 1 = 0$ *Answer(s):* _____

8. $3 \cot^2 \theta + 2 \csc \theta - 5 = 0$ *Answer(s):* _____

9. $\tan^2 \theta + 10 \sec \theta + 10 = 0$ *Answer(s):* _____

10. $5 \sec^2 \theta + 2 \tan \theta - 21 = 0$ *Answer(s):* _____

15

Solving Trigonometric Equations—Part 3

In this lesson, we will explore the techniques that are used to solve equations that contain **double angle formulas involving trigonometric ratios**. In order to solve some of these equations, we will need to use a trigonometric identity that allows us to rewrite the equation with trigonometric ratios that have only single angles.

Your Goal: When you have completed this lesson, you should be able to solve for the value(s) of an unknown angle in equations that contain trigonometric ratios that involve double angles.

As in Lessons 13 and 14 we will only be concerned with trigonometric ratios of angles that lie between 0° and 360°, inclusive. Also, θ will represent the unknown angle.

Solving Trigonometric Equations— Part 3

We start with the notation sin 2θ. In order to evaluate this expression, we first double the angle value, then apply the sine ratio. For example, if θ = 25°, then sin 2θ = sin 50° ≈ 0.7660. Note that the value of 2 sin θ, given that θ = 25°, is 2 sin 25° ≈ (2)(0.4226) = 0.8452.

For nearly all values of θ, sin 2θ ≠ 2 sin θ. In a similar way, we can demonstrate that, except for rare exceptions, cos 2θ ≠ 2 cos θ. This concept can also be extended to the other four trigonometric ratios.

MathFlash!

For an expression such as sin 2θ, we are limiting the trigonometric ratio to angles whose measures are less than 360°. For this reason, our answers for θ will be less than 180°.

1 **Example:** *What is (are) the value(s) of θ in the equation sin 2θ + 0.27 = 4 sin 2θ?*

Solution: First subtract sin 2θ from each side to get 0.27 = 3 sin 2θ.
Dividing by 3 leads to 0.09 = sin 2θ.
Then 2θ = sin⁻¹(0.09) ≈ 5.2° or 174.8°.
Finally, divide by 2 so that θ ≈ 3° or 87°.

MathFlash!

When evaluating sin⁻¹(0.09), be sure to find <u>both</u> angles that satisfy this requirement. Then determine the value of θ from each of these angle measures. Note that we rounded off the value of sin⁻¹(0.09) to the nearest tenth. In this way, we get a more accurate estimate of the value of θ to the nearest degree.

2 **Example:** *What is (are) the value(s) of θ in the equation cot 2θ + 2 = –1.6?*

Solution: Subtract 4 from each side to get cot 2θ = –3.6.
Then 2θ = cot⁻¹(–3.6) ≈ 164.5° or 344.5°.
Thus, θ ≈ 82° or 172°.

3 **Example:** *What is (are) the value(s) of θ in the equation 5 sec 2θ – 9 = 2(sec 2θ – 7)?*

Solution: Removing parentheses, the equation becomes
5 sec 2θ – 9 = 2 sec 2θ – 14.
Bringing all terms containing sec 2θ to the left side and numbers to the right side, the equation further simplifies to 3 sec 2θ = –5.

Then $2\theta = \sec^{-1}\left(-\dfrac{5}{3}\right) \approx 126.9°$ or 233.1°.

Thus, θ ≈ 63° or 117°.

4 **Example:** *What is (are) the value(s) of θ in the equation tan² 2θ – 9 tan 2θ + 20 = 0?*

Solution: Just a friendly reminder that in order to evaluate tan² 2θ, we <u>first</u> double the angle value, <u>then</u> find the tangent value, and <u>finally</u> square this number. For example, if θ = 35°, then
tan² 2θ = tan²(70°) ≈ (2.7475)² ≈ 7.5487.

Returning to the given equation, factor the left side so that the equation becomes (tan 2θ – 5)(tan 2θ – 4) = 0.
If tan 2θ – 5 = 0, then 2θ = tan⁻¹(5) ≈ 78.7° or 258.7°.
Thus, θ ≈ 39° or 129°.
If tan 2θ – 4 = 0, then 2θ = tan⁻¹(4) ≈ 76.0° or 256.0°.
Thus, θ ≈ 38° or 128°.
Our four answers are 38°, 39°, 128°, and 129°.

5 **Example:** *What is (are) the value(s) of θ in the equation*
3 csc² 2θ + 7 csc 2θ + 2 = 0?

Solution: By factoring the left side, the equation becomes
$(3 \csc 2\theta + 1)(\csc 2\theta + 2) = 0$.

If $3 \csc 2\theta + 1 = 0$, then $2\theta = \csc^{-1}\left(-\dfrac{1}{3}\right)$, which is impossible.

If $\csc 2\theta + 2 = 0$, then $2\theta = \csc^{-1}(-2) = 210°$ or $330°$.
Thus, $\theta = 105°$ or $165°$.

There are also **popular double-angle formulas** for the sine and cosine ratios. Each of these formulas shows a connection between, for example, sin 2θ and sin θ. (You can verify the formulas by substituting a value of θ.)

Our <u>first</u> double-angle formula is **sin 2θ = 2 sin θ cos θ**. You would use this formula to solve an equation that contained both sin 2θ and sin θ <u>or</u> both sin 2θ and cos θ.

6 **Example:** *What is (are) the value(s) of θ in the equation 10 sin θ + sin 2θ = 0?*

Solution: Be sure that you do <u>not</u> write sin 2θ as just 2 sin θ!
Using the <u>correct</u> substitution, we can write this equation as
$10 \sin \theta + 2 \sin \theta \cos \theta = 0$.
Next, use Common Term factoring to get $(2 \sin \theta)(5 + \cos \theta) = 0$.
If $2 \sin \theta = 0$, then $\theta = 0°$ or $180°$.
If $5 + \cos \theta = 0$, then $\theta = \cos^{-1}(-5)$, which does not exist.
The only two answers are 0° or 180°.

7 **Example:** *What is (are) the value(s) of θ in the equation 5 cos θ − 4 sin 2θ = 0?*

Solution: By substituting 2 sin θ cos θ for sin 2θ, the equation
becomes $5 \cos \theta - (4)(2 \sin \theta \cos \theta) = 0$, which simplifies
to $5 \cos \theta - 8 \sin \theta \cos \theta = 0$.
Now, Common Term factoring gives us $(\cos \theta)(5 - 8 \sin \theta) = 0$.
If $\cos \theta = 0$, then $\theta = \cos^{-1}(0) = 90°$ or $270°$.

If $5 - 8 \sin \theta = 0$, then $\theta = \sin^{-1}\left(\dfrac{5}{8}\right) \approx 39°$ or $141°$.

Our <u>second</u> double-angle formula is **cos 2θ = 2 cos² θ – 1 = 1 – 2 sin² θ**. You would use cos 2θ = 2 cos² θ – 1 to solve an equation that contains <u>both</u> cos θ and cos 2θ. You would use cos 2θ = 1 – 2 sin² θ to solve an equation that contains <u>both</u> sin θ and cos 2θ.

8 **Example:** *What is (are) the value(s) of θ in the equation cos 2θ + cos θ = 0?*

   Solution: Let's substitute 2 cos² θ – 1 for cos 2θ to get 2 cos² θ – 1 + cos θ = 0.
   Switching the second and third terms, 2 cos² θ + cos θ – 1 = 0.
   Trial and Error factoring allows us to write (2 cos θ – 1)(cos θ + 1) = 0.

   If 2 cos θ – 1 = 0, then $\theta = \cos^{-1}\left(\dfrac{1}{2}\right) = 60°$ or 300°.

   If cos θ + 1 = 0, then θ = cos⁻¹(–1) = 180°.

MathFlash!

If you wanted to check the answer of 300° in Example 8, your equation would be cos 600° + cos 300° = 0. Although we have never discussed the trigonometric ratios for angles above 360°, your calculator will display a value of –0.5 for cos 600°. Since cos 300° = 0.5, the answer of 300° does check out.

9 **Example:** *What is (are) the value(s) of θ in the equation 3 cos 2θ + 11 cos θ + 6 = 0?*

   Solution: We should substitute 2 cos² θ – 1 for cos 2θ to get
   3(2 cos² θ – 1) + 11 cos θ + 6 = 0.
   Now remove the parentheses and combine similar terms to get 6 cos² θ + 11 cos θ + 3 = 0.
   Trial and Error factoring leads to (3 cos θ + 1)(2 cos θ +3) = 0.

   If 3 cos θ + 1 = 0, then $\theta = \cos^{-1}\left(-\dfrac{1}{3}\right) \approx 109°$ or 251°.

   If 2 cos θ + 3 = 0, then $\theta = \cos^{-1}\left(-\dfrac{3}{2}\right)$, which does not exist.

   The only two answers are 109° or 251°.

10 **Example:** *What is (are) the value(s) of θ in the equation cos 2θ − 5 sin θ + 2 = 0?*

Solution: Let's substitute $1 - 2 \sin^2 \theta$ for cos 2θ to get
$1 - 2 \sin^2 \theta - 5 \sin \theta + 2 = 0$.
After combining the first and last terms to get 3, multiply the entire equation by −1 to get $2 \sin^2 \theta + 5 \sin \theta - 3 = 0$.
Factor this equation so that it becomes $(2 \sin \theta - 1)(\sin \theta + 3 = 0) = 0$.

If $2 \sin \theta - 1 = 0$, then $\theta = \sin^{-1}\left(\dfrac{1}{2}\right) = 30°$ or $150°$.

If $\sin \theta + 3 = 0$, then $\theta = \sin^{-1}(-3)$, which is impossible.

11 **Example:** *What is (are) the value(s) of θ in the equation
3 cos 2θ + 22 sin² θ − 4 = 0?*

Solution: This appears to be just a tad harder than Example 10, but we should still replace cos 2θ with $1 - 2 \sin^2 \theta$ to get
$3(1 - 2 \sin^2 \theta) + 22 \sin^2 \theta - 4 = 0$.
Removing the parentheses leads to $3 - 6 \sin^2 \theta + 22 \sin^2 \theta - 4 = 0$.
Combining similar terms reduces this equation to $16 \sin^2 \theta - 1 = 0$.
This equation type should look very familiar!
Using the Difference of Two Squares factoring, we get
$(4 \sin \theta - 1)(4 \sin \theta + 1) = 0$. If $4 \sin \theta - 1 = 0$, then

$\theta = \sin^{-1}\left(\dfrac{1}{4}\right) \approx 15°$ or $165°$.

If $4 \sin \theta + 1 = 0$, then $\theta = \sin^{-1}\left(-\dfrac{1}{4}\right) \approx 195°$ or $345°$.

For each problem, determine the value(s) of θ for which the equation is true. Each equation has at least one solution.

1. $7 \tan 2\theta + 1.5 = 4 \tan 2\theta$ *Answer(s):* _____

2. $3 \sec 2\theta + 4.3 = 2 \sec 2\theta + 6.5$ *Answer(s):* _____

3. $10 \sin 2\theta - 5 = -8.4$ *Answer(s):* _____

4. $8 \cot 2\theta - 3 = 5 (\cot 2\theta + 1.2)$ *Answer(s):* _____

5. $\csc^2 2\theta - 5 \csc 2\theta - 14 = 0$ *Answer(s):* _____

6. $6 \cos \theta + 5 \sin 2\theta = 0$ *Answer(s):* _____

7. $4 \sin 2\theta - 3 \sin \theta = 0$ *Answer(s):* _____

8. $6 \cot^2 2\theta - 19 \cot 2\theta + 15 = 0$ *Answer(s):* _____

9. $4 \cos 2\theta - 6 \cos \theta - 1 = 0$ *Answer(s):* _____

10. $2 \cos 2\theta + 13 \sin^2 \theta - 3 = 0$ *Answer(s):* _____

LESSONS 13-15

QUIZ FOUR

What is (are) the value(s) of θ that satisfy the given equation in each question? (Answers should be rounded off to the nearest degree.)

1. $4 \cot \theta - \dfrac{\tan \theta}{3} = 0$

   A Only 74° or 254°

   B 74°, 106°, 254°, or 286°

   C Only 85° or 265°

   D 85°, 95°, 265°, or 275°

2. $\sec^2 \theta - 7 \sec \theta - 8 = 0$

   A 0°, 83°, or 277°

   B 83°, 180°, or 277°

   C 0°, 97° or 263°

   D 97°, 180°, or 263°

3. $2 \cos 2\theta + 5 \cos \theta - 4 = 0$

   A 41° or 319°

   B 76° or 284°

   C 104° or 256°

   D 139° or 221°

4. $2 \csc \theta + 6.3 = -1.5$

   A 15° or 165°

   B 25° or 155°

   C 195° or 345°

   D 205° or 335°

5. $4 \tan^2 \theta + \tan \theta = 0$

   A 0°, 141°, 180°, or 321°

   B 0°, 166°, 180°, or 346°

   C 0°, 39°, 180°, or 219°

   D 0°, 14°, 180°, or 194°

6. $3 \sin^2 \theta + 3 \cos^2 \theta - 7 \cos \theta = 0$

   A Only 115° or 245°

   B 90°, 115°, 245°, or 270°

   C Only 65° or 295°

   D 65°, 90°, 270°, or 295°

7. $3.5 \csc 2\theta - 9 = \csc 2\theta - 6$

   A 236° or 304°

   B 118° or 152°

   C 56° or 124°

   D 28° or 62°

8. $6 \tan^2 \theta + 13 \sec \theta + 1 = 0$

   A 127° or 233°

   B 114° or 246°

   C 66° or 294°

   D 53° or 307°

9. $2 \csc^2 \theta + 7 \cot \theta - 2 = 0$

   A 0°, 16°, 180°, or 196°

   B 0°, 164°, 180°, or 344°

   C 16°, 90°, 196°, or 270°

   D 90°, 164°, 270°, or 344°

10. $100 \cos^2 \theta - 9 = 0$

    A 73°, 107°, 253°, or 287°

    B Only 73° or 287°

    C 85°, 95°, 265°, or 275°

    D Only 85° or 275°

CUMULATIVE EXAM

All answers for angles in degree measure are to be rounded off to the nearest degree. All answers for lengths in figures are rounded off to the nearest hundredth.

1. What are the values of θ in the equation $3 \cos^2 \theta + 4 \cos \theta = 0$?

   A 90°, 139°, 221°, or 270°

   B 0°, 41°, 180°, or 319°

   C 90° or 270°

   D 0° or 180°

2. What are the values of θ in the equation $9 \cot 2\theta = 2(\cot 2\theta - 3)$?

   A 65° or 147°

   B 57° or 147°

   C 65° or 155°

   D 57° or 155°

3. If $\tan \theta = \dfrac{3}{11}$ and θ lies in the third quadrant, then what is the value of cot θ?

   A $-\dfrac{3}{11}$

   B $\dfrac{11}{3}$

   C $\dfrac{3}{11}$ or $-\dfrac{3}{11}$

   D $\dfrac{11}{3}$ or $-\dfrac{11}{3}$

4. Given that θ is an angle that is measured in radians and that $\pi < \theta < \dfrac{3\pi}{2}$, which one of the following is true?

   A $\cos \theta = \cos(\theta - \pi)$

   B $\cos \theta = -\cos(\theta - \pi)$

   C $\cos(\theta + \pi) = -\cos(\theta - \pi)$

   D $\cos(\theta + \pi) = \cos(\theta + \dfrac{\pi}{2})$

5. Which one of the following conditions describes a quadrantal angle in standard position?

   A Its initial ray lies on the positive x-axis and its terminal ray lies on the x-axis or on the y-axis.

   B Its initial ray lies on the negative x-axis and its terminal ray lies on the x-axis or on the y-axis.

   C Its initial ray lies on the positive x-axis and its terminal ray does not lie on any axis.

   D Its initial ray lies on the negative x-axis and its terminal ray does not lie on any axis.

6. Kelli and Robert leave their place of employment at the same time. Kelli is walking north at 4.5 miles per hour, while Robert is walking east at 3.6 miles per hour. After 4 hours, approximately how many miles apart will they be?

    A 20.45

    B 23.05

    C 25.65

    D 28.25

7. Consider △VWX, as shown below.

    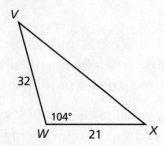

    What is the value of VX?

    A 42.31

    B 39.46

    C 36.61

    D 33.76

8. In addition to 90° and 270°, what are the values of θ in the equation $8 \cos \theta + 7 \sin 2\theta = 0$?

    A 35° or 145°

    B 61° or 119°

    C 215° or 325°

    D 241° or 299°

9. Consider △BEH, as shown below.

    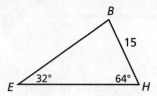

    What is the value of EH?

    A 28.15

    B 29.85

    C 31.55

    D 33.25

10. The minute hand of a clock is pointing to the number 12. If the minute hand rotates exactly two radians, which number is the closest to where it will point?

    A 1

    B 2

    C 3

    D 4

11. A 44-foot ladder is leaning against the side of a building. The bottom of the ladder is 33 feet from the bottom of the building. What is the angle of elevation of the ladder?

    A 75°

    B 58°

    C 41°

    D 24°

12. Which one of the following has the
    exact value of $\dfrac{1}{\sqrt{3}}$?

    A tan 60°

    B cot 60°

    C sin 35°

    D csc 55°

13. In △*PRT*, the measure of ∠*P* is 25°,
    RT = 15, and *PT* = 28. Given that
    ∠*R* is an obtuse angle, what is
    the measure of ∠*T*?

    A 128°

    B 103°

    C 52°

    D 27°

14. Which one of the following
    equations has <u>no</u> solution for θ?

    A csc θ + 2.5 = 3.3

    B cot θ + 2.5 = −3.3

    C cos θ + 3.3 = 2.5

    D sin θ − 3.3 = −2.5

15. What are the values of θ in the
    equation $5\cot\theta - \dfrac{\tan\theta}{2} = 0$?

    A 72°, 108°, 252°, or 288°

    B 66°, 114°, 246°, or 294°

    C 60°, 120°, 240°, or 300°

    D 54°, 126°, 234°, or 306°

16. What is the area of a triangle with
    sides whose lengths are 10, 13,
    and 17?

    A 52.21

    B 56.41

    C 60.61

    D 64.81

17. Ramona is standing on the top of
    a vertical cliff next to a river. She is
    looking at a steamboat that is 550
    feet from the bottom of the cliff. If
    the angle of depression is 16°, what
    is the height of the cliff?

    A 143.31 feet

    B 148.11 feet

    C 152.91 feet

    D 157.71 feet

18. What are the values of θ in the
    following equation?
    $9\sin^2\theta + 16\cos\theta + 9\cos^2\theta = 0$

    A 124° or 236°

    B 139° or 221°

    C 41° or 319°

    D 56° or 304°

19. In the figure below, ∠K is a right angle.

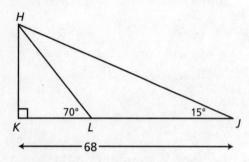

What is the value of *HL*?

A 18.22

B 19.39

C 20.56

D 21.73

20. In the figure below, both ∠MQN and ∠MQP are right angles.

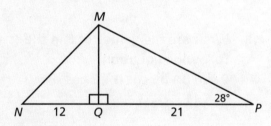

What is the measure of ∠N?

A 43°

B 39°

C 35°

D 31°

21. Which one of the following is not equivalent to the other three answer choices?

A sec 180° = −1

B sec 1° = 180

C sec⁻¹(−1) = 180°

D 180° represents an angle whose secant ratio is equal to −1.

22. In rhombus *QRST*, *QR* = 18 and diagonal *QS* = 14. What is the measure of ∠R?

A 42°

B 44°

C 46°

D 48°

23. If θ lies in the second quadrant and sec² θ ≈ 2.4025, then what is the best approximation for the value of tan θ?

A 1.40

B 1.18

C −1.18

D −1.40

24. In the figure below, ∠Z is a right angle.

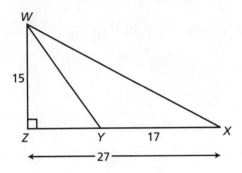

What is the measure of ∠WYX?

A 151°

B 142°

C 133°

D 124°

25. In rectangle *ADGJ*, *DG* = 7 and the measure of ∠*DGA* is 77°. What is the length of either diagonal?

A 33.42

B 31.12

C 28.82

D 26.52

Answer Key

1. 216° $\left(\dfrac{6\pi}{5}\right)\left(\dfrac{180}{\pi}\right)$

2. 180° Definition of a straight angle.

3. C In quadrant II, each *x*-coordinate is negative and each *y*-coordinate is positive.

4. A The point must lie on either the *x*-axis or the *y*-axis. Thus, at least one coordinate must be zero.

5. $\dfrac{3\pi}{4}$ radians $(135)\left(\dfrac{\pi}{180}\right)$

6. B A reflex angle is greater than 180° but less than 360°.

7. 150° $(360°)\left(\dfrac{5}{12}\right)$

8. C If an angle is named with three letters, the middle letter must be the vertex.

9. 171.9° $\left(\dfrac{180}{\pi}\right)(3)$

10. $\dfrac{3\pi}{2}$ radians $(2\pi)\left(\dfrac{9}{12}\right)$

Lessons

2

1. D — The initial ray must lie on the positive *x*-axis and the terminal ray must lie on the *x*-axis or on the *y*-axis.

2. C — Definition of a positive angle.

3. A — The sine ratio is $\dfrac{\text{opposite side}}{\text{hypotenuse}}$.

4. 0.3584 — Calculator reading

5. 0.9848 — Calculator reading

6. D — For any angle in standard position, the initial ray must lie on the positive *x*-axis.

7. 6.26 — $(45)(\sin 8°)$

8. 9.54 — $(18)\left(\sin \dfrac{8\pi}{45}\right)$

9. 78.81 — $\dfrac{72}{\sin 66°}$

10. 58.25 — $\dfrac{49}{\sin \dfrac{7\pi}{22}}$

3

1. 0.3546 — Calculator reading

2. C — $\cos 150° = \cos 210° \approx -0.8660$.

3. 18° — $360° - 342°$

4. D — $\cos \dfrac{12\pi}{7} = \cos \dfrac{2\pi}{7} \approx 0.6235$.

5. B — Definition of the cosine ratio.

6. B — The cosine ratio is positive in the first and fourth quadrants. It is negative in the second and third quadrants.

7. 15.64 — $(20)\left(\cos \dfrac{3\pi}{14}\right)$

8. 50.23 — $\dfrac{13}{\cos 75°}$

9. 37.17 — $(38)(\cos 12°)$

10. 9.62 — $\dfrac{6}{\cos \dfrac{2\pi}{7}}$

Lessons

4

1. C The tangent ratio is positive in the first and third quadrants.

2. B For any angle in the fourth quadrant, $\tan\theta = -\tan(2\pi - \theta)$.

3. A $\tan 162° = \tan 342° \approx -0.3249$

4. 35.94 $\dfrac{16}{\tan 24°}$

5. 20.78 $(12)\left(\tan\dfrac{\pi}{3}\right)$

6. 0.5317 $\tan\theta = \dfrac{\sin\theta}{\cos\theta} = \dfrac{-0.4695}{-0.8830}$.

7. D $\sin^2\theta = 1 - \cos^2\theta = 1 - \left(\dfrac{3}{7}\right)^2 \approx 0.8163$.

$\sin\theta = -\sqrt{0.8163}$, since θ is in the fourth quadrant.

8. D Draw a right triangle in the third quadrant. The hypotenuse equals

$\sqrt{5^2 + 8^2} = \sqrt{89}$. Then $\sin\theta = -\dfrac{8}{\sqrt{89}}$, since θ is in the third quadrant.

9. B If $\sin\theta = -\dfrac{2}{5}$, then $\cos^2\theta = 1 - \left(-\dfrac{2}{5}\right)^2 = 0.84$. Thus, $\cos\theta = \pm\sqrt{0.84} \neq -\dfrac{4}{5}$.

10. C For any angle θ, at least one of $\sin\theta$, $\cos\theta$, or $\tan\theta$ must be positive.

Lessons

5

1. $-\dfrac{10}{9}$

$\csc \theta = \dfrac{1}{\sin \theta} = \dfrac{1}{-\dfrac{9}{10}}$.

2. 2.1113 or –2.1113

$\tan^2 \theta = \sec^2 \theta - 1 = (-2.3362)^2 - 1 \approx 4.4578$.

If θ is in quadrant II, $\tan \theta = -\sqrt{4.4578}$.

If θ is in quadrant III, $\tan \theta = \sqrt{4.4578}$.

3. –2.0765

$\cot \dfrac{6\pi}{7} = \dfrac{1}{\tan \dfrac{6\pi}{7}} = \dfrac{1}{-0.4816}$.

4. 0.7332

$\cot^2 \theta = \csc^2 \theta - 1 = (1.24)^2 - 1 = 0.5376$.

$\cot \theta = \sqrt{0.5376}$.

5. Quadrant II

In the second quadrant, the tangent ratio is negative and the cosecant ratio is positive.

6. D

Since the sine and cosecant ratios are reciprocals of each other, they must be either both positive or both negative.

7. $\dfrac{15}{17}$

The hypotenuse of the right triangle is 17 and the adjacent side is 8. The opposite side is $\sqrt{17^2 - 8^2} = \sqrt{225} = 15$.

$\sin \theta = \dfrac{\text{opposite side}}{\text{hypotenuse}}$.

8. –1.4821

$\cot \theta = \dfrac{\cos \theta}{\sin \theta} = \dfrac{-0.83}{0.56}$.

9. 1.0271 or –1.0271

$\csc^2 \theta = \cot^2 \theta + 1 = (0.2345)^2 + 1 \approx 1.0550$. $\csc \theta = \pm\sqrt{1.0550}$.

10. B

The approximate values of answer choices A, B, C, and D are –3.08, 2.08, 0.98, and 1.74 respectively.

Lessons

6

1. 34° $\cos \theta = \sin(90° - \theta)$, so $\theta = 90° - 56°$.

2. B $\csc 270° = \dfrac{1}{\sin 270°} = \dfrac{1}{-1}$.

3. One $\tan \dfrac{3\pi}{2}$ is not defined.

4. D   Each of tan 45° and cot 45° equals 1.

5. 298°   If θ is an acute angle, then $\sec \theta = \sec(360° - \theta) = \sec(360° - 62°)$.

6. $\dfrac{3\pi}{4}$ If θ is in the fourth quadrant, then $\cot \theta = \cot(\theta - \pi) = \cot\left(\dfrac{7\pi}{4} - \pi\right)$.

7. Two   Each of the sine ratio and cosecant ratio has a negative value in the third and fourth quadrants.

8. 353°   The reference angle for 97° is 83°. cos 83° = sin(90° − 83°) = sin 7°.
            Then 360° − 7° is the fourth quadrant angle whose reference angle is 7°.

9. $\dfrac{14\pi}{15}$ If θ is in the first quadrant, then $\csc \theta = \csc(\pi - \theta) = \csc \theta \left(\pi - \dfrac{\pi}{15}\right)$.

10. 144°   The reference angle for 306° is 54°. Then, sin 54° = cos(90° − 54°) = cos 36°.
             Then 180° − 36° is the second quadrant angle whose reference angle is 36°.

Lessons

7

1. 59° or 239°   Calculator reading for 59°.
   The third quadrant angle is 180° + 59°.

2. 150° or 210°   Calculator reading for $\cos^{-1}\left(\dfrac{\sqrt{3}}{2}\right)$ is 30°. The values of
   $\cos^{-1}\left(-\dfrac{\sqrt{3}}{2}\right)$ are in the second and third quadrants.
   They are given by 180° − 30° and 180° + 30°.

3. 22° or 158° $\csc^{-1}(2.65) = \sin^{-1}\left(\dfrac{1}{2.65}\right) \approx \sin^{-1}(0.3774)$.

4. 135° or 225° $\sec^{-1}(-1.42) = \cos^{-1}\left(-\dfrac{1}{1.42}\right) \approx \cos^{-1}(-0.7042)$.
   Since $\cos^{-1}(0.7042) \approx 45°$, the values of $\cos^{-1}(-0.7042)$
   are given by 180° − 45° and 180° + 45°.

5. 304°   Calculator reading for $\cos^{-1}\left(\dfrac{5}{9}\right) \approx 56°$.
   The fourth quadrant angle is 360° − 56°.

6. 111° $\cot^{-1}(-0.38) = \tan^{-1}\left(-\dfrac{1}{0.38}\right) \approx \tan^{-1}(-2.63)$.
   Since $\tan^{-1}(2.63) \approx 69°$, the second quadrant angle
   for $\tan^{-1}(-2.63)$ is 180° − 69°.

7. 198°   Since $\sin^{-1}\left(\dfrac{5}{16}\right) \approx 18°$, the third quadrant angle for
   $\sin^{-1}\left(-\dfrac{5}{16}\right)$ is 180° + 18°.

8. 147° $\csc^{-1}(1.85) = \sin^{-1}\left(\dfrac{1}{1.85}\right) \approx \sin^{-1}(0.54) \approx 33°$.
   The corresponding second quadrant angle is 180° − 33°.

9. A   tan(−1) = 315° is meaningless. By definition, each of answer
   choices B, C, and D is equivalent to tan(315°) = −1.

10. C $\sec^{-1} x$ is defined only for $x \geq 1$ or for $x \leq -1$.

8

1. 25.69 $a^2 = 27^2 - 8.3^2 = 729 - 68.89 = 660.11.$ $a = \sqrt{660.11}.$

2. 40° $\angle A = \sin^{-1}\left(\dfrac{11}{17}\right).$

3. 96.16 $a = \dfrac{35}{\tan 20°}.$

4. 12.58 $b = (48.6)(\cos 75°).$

5. 35°   Angle of elevation is $\tan^{-1}\left(\dfrac{45}{65}\right).$

6. 63°   Angle of elevation is $\cos^{-1}\left(\dfrac{25}{56}\right).$

7. 136.10 feet   Length of wire is $\dfrac{80}{\sin 36°}.$

8. 178.09 feet   Height of cliff is $(400)(\tan 24°).$

9. 19.56 miles   After 3 hours, the distances walked are 10.5 miles and 16.5 miles. The distance between them is $\sqrt{10.5^2 + 16.5^2} = \sqrt{382.5}.$

10. 60.79 miles per hour   Let x represent Jeff's speed. After 2 hours, Rachel's distance is 104 miles and Jeff's distance is $2x$ miles. Then $(2x)^2 + 104^2 = 160^2$. This equation simplifies to $4x^2 + 10{,}816 = 25{,}600$, which further simplifies to $4x^2 = 14{,}784$. So $x^2 = \dfrac{14{,}784}{4} = 3696.$ Thus, $x = \sqrt{3696}.$

Lessons

9

1. 0.79 $FG = (19)(\sin 40°) \approx 12.21$. $GH = 13 - 12.21$.

2. 58° $EF = (23)(\sin 15°) \approx 5.95$. $\angle FEG = \tan^{-1}\left(\dfrac{9.5}{5.95}\right)$.

3. 12° $FG^2 = 31^2 - 10^2 = 961 - 100 = 861$. Therefore, $FG = \sqrt{861} \approx 29.34$.
$FH = 29.34 + 16 = 45.34$. Then $\angle H = \tan^{-1}\left(\dfrac{10}{45.34}\right)$.

4. 29.53 $\angle EGF = 180° - 125° = 55°$. $EF = (11)(\tan 55°) \approx 15.71$.
Then $EH^2 = 15.71^2 + 25^2 = 246.80 + 625 = 871.80$.
Then, $EH = \sqrt{871.80}$.

5. 120° $FH = \sqrt{32^2 + 21^2} = \sqrt{583} \approx 24.15$. $FG = 24.15 - 12 = 12.15$.
$\angle EGF = \tan^{-1}\left(\dfrac{21}{12.15}\right) \approx 60°$. Then $\angle EGH = 180° - 60°$.

6. 53.19 $EF = (60)(\tan 39°) \approx 48.59$. $EG = \dfrac{48.59}{\sin 66°}$.

7. 62° $JL = (28)(\tan 25°) \approx 13.06$. $\angle K = \tan^{-1}\left(\dfrac{13.06}{7}\right)$.

8. 20.47 $JL = (52)(\sin 16°) \approx 14.33$. $KL = \dfrac{14.33}{\tan 35°}$.

9. 11.13 $KL = (55)(\sin 74°) \approx 52.87$. $LM = 64 - 52.87$.

10. 71° $JL = \sqrt{30^2 - 19^2} = \sqrt{539} \approx 23.22$. $\angle LJM = \cos^{-1}\left(\dfrac{23.22}{72}\right)$.

Lessons

10

1. 15.25 $\angle A = 180° - 48° - 48° - 34° = 98°.$ $\dfrac{27}{\sin 98°} = \dfrac{c}{\sin 34°}$.

Then $c = \dfrac{(27)(\sin 34°)}{\sin 98°}$.

2. 54.14 $\dfrac{a}{\sin 73°} = \dfrac{30}{\sin 32°}$. Then $a = \dfrac{(30)(\sin 73°)}{\sin 32°}$.

3. 35° $\dfrac{12}{\sin \angle A} = \dfrac{19}{\sin 65°}$. $(12)(\sin 65°) = (19)(\sin \angle A).$

$\sin \angle A = \dfrac{(12)(\sin 65°)}{19} \approx 0.5724$.

Then $\angle A = \sin^{-1}(0.5724).$

4. 24° $\dfrac{33}{\sin \angle B} = \dfrac{42}{\sin 108°}$. $\sin \angle B = \dfrac{(33)(\sin 108°)}{42} \approx 0.7473$.

$\angle B = \sin^{-1}(0.7473) \approx 48°.$ Then $\angle C = 180° - 108° - 48°.$

5. 13.32 $\dfrac{DJ}{\sin 56°} = \dfrac{16}{\sin 85°}$. Then $DJ = \dfrac{(16)(\sin 56°)}{\sin 85°}$.

6. 48.17 $K = 180° - 122° - 25° = 33°.$

$\dfrac{MP}{\sin 33°} = \dfrac{75}{\sin 122°}$.

Then $MP = \dfrac{(75)(\sin 33°)}{\sin 122°}$.

7. 49° $\dfrac{21}{\sin \angle V} = \dfrac{28}{\sin 83°}$.

$\sin \angle V = \dfrac{(21)(\sin 83°)}{28} \approx 0.7444$.

$\angle V = \sin^{-1}(0.7444) \approx 48°.$

Then $\angle Q = 180° - 83° - 48°.$

Lessons

10
(cont.)

8. 165°

$$\frac{48}{\sin \angle Z} = \frac{39}{\sin 12°}.$$

$$\sin \angle Z = \frac{(48)(\sin 12°)}{39} \approx 0.2559.$$

$\angle Z = \sin^{-1}(0.2559) \approx 165°$, since $\angle Z$ is an obtuse angle.

9. 21.61

$\angle E = 180° - 23° - 76° = 81°. \quad \dfrac{22}{\sin 81°} = \dfrac{EK}{\sin 76°}.$

Then $EK = \dfrac{(22)(\sin 76°)}{\sin 81°}.$

10. 8°

$$\frac{70}{\sin 152°} = \frac{20}{\sin \angle N}.$$

$$\sin \angle N = \frac{(20)(\sin 152°)}{70} \approx 0.1341.$$

Then $\angle N = \sin^{-1}(0.1341).$

11

1. 15.87

$b^2 = 20^2 + 17^2 - (2)(20)(17)(\cos 50°)$
$= 400 + 289 - (680)(\cos 50°) \approx 251.90.$
Then $b = \sqrt{251.90}.$

2. 17°

$8^2 = 19^2 + 24^2 - (2)(19)(24)(\cos \angle C).$
$64 = 381 + 576 - (912)(\cos \angle C).$
$-873 = (-912)(\cos \angle C).$
Then $\angle C = \cos^{-1}\left(\dfrac{873}{912}\right) \approx \cos^{-1}(0.9572).$

3. 57.54

$a^2 = 40^2 + 35^2 - (2)(40)(35)(\cos 100°)$
$= 1600 + 1225 - (2800)(\cos 100°) \approx 3311.21$
Then $a = \sqrt{3311.21}.$

Lessons

4. 56°

$25^2 = 30^2 + 15^2 - (2)(30(15)(\cos \angle K)$.
$625 = 900 + 225 - (900)(\cos \angle K)$.
$-500 = (-900)(\cos \angle K)$.
Then $\angle K = \cos^{-1}\left(\dfrac{500}{900}\right) \approx \cos^{-1}(0.5556)$.

5. 25°

$18^2 = 36^2 + 42^2 - (2)(36)(42)(\cos \angle F)$.
$324 = 1296 + 1764 - (3024)(\cos \angle F)$.
$-2736 = (-3024)(\cos \angle F)$.
Then $\angle F = \cos^{-1}\left(\dfrac{2736}{3024}\right) \approx \cos^{-1}(0.9048)$.

6. 19.16

$(GJ)^2 = 9^2 + 16^2 - (2)(9)(16)(\cos 96°)$
$= 81 + 256 - (288)(\cos 96°) \approx 367.10$.
Then $GJ = \sqrt{367.10}$.

7. 130.22

Semi-perimeter = 26.435.
Area $= \sqrt{(26.435)(6.435)(9.435)(10.565)} \approx \sqrt{16{,}956.6}$.

8. 187.08

Semi-perimeter = 35.
Area $= \sqrt{(35)(20)(10)(5)} = \sqrt{35{,}000}$.

9. 81.61

Semi-perimeter = 24.5.
Area $= \sqrt{(24.5)(14.5)(7.5)(2.5)} = \sqrt{6660.9}$.

10. 923.50

$ST = \sqrt{50^2 + 60^2 - (2)(50)(60)(\cos 38°)} \approx \sqrt{1371.9} \approx 37.04$.
Semi-perimeter = 73.52.
Area $= \sqrt{(73.52)(23.52)(13.52)(36.48)} \approx \sqrt{852{,}853.3}$.

Lessons

12

1. 21.21 $EG = \sqrt{15^2 + 15^2} = \sqrt{450}$.

2. 16.70 $LM = \sqrt{20^2 - 11^2} = \sqrt{279}$.

3. 33° $\angle KML = \sin^{-1}\left(\dfrac{11}{20}\right)$.

4. 63.56 $QS = (50)(\sin 19°) \approx 16.28$.
   $QT = (50)(\cos 19°) \approx 47.28$.
   $16.28 + 47.28$.

5. 36° $62^2 = 100^2 + 62^2 - (2)(100)(62)(\cos \angle VXY)$.
   $\cos \angle VXY = \dfrac{10,000}{12,400} \approx 0.8065$.
   $\angle VXY = \cos^{-1}(0.8065)$.

6. 108° $\angle XVY = \angle VXY = 36°$.
   $\angle Y = 180° - 36° - 36°$

7. 42.08 $BF = \sqrt{48^2 + 48^2 - (2)(48)(48)(\cos 52°)} \approx \sqrt{1771}$.

8. 124° $18^2 = 21^2 + 16^2 - (2)(21)(16)(\cos \angle J)$.
   $\cos \angle J = \dfrac{373}{672}$. $\angle J \approx 56°$.
   $\angle JLN = 180° - 56°$.

9. 60.65 $RV = \sqrt{33^2 + 40^2 - (2)(33)(40)(\cos 112°)} \approx \sqrt{3677.96}$.

10. 87° $\dfrac{20}{\sin \angle WZX} = \dfrac{14}{\sin 36°}$.
    $\sin \angle WZX = \dfrac{(20)(\sin 36°)}{14} \approx 0.8397$.
    $\angle WZX \approx 57°$. $\angle WXZ = 180° - 36° - 57°$.

13

1. 41° or 319°
$$\cos\theta=\frac{8-5}{4}.\ \theta=\cos^{-1}\left(\frac{3}{4}\right).$$

2. 160° or 340°
$$\cot\theta=-2.75.\ \theta=\cot^{-1}(-2.75)\approx\tan^{-1}(-0.36).$$

3. 243° or 297°
$$8\sin\theta-8=17\sin\theta.\ \sin\theta=-\frac{8}{9}.\ \theta=\sin^{-1}\left(-\frac{8}{9}\right).$$

4. 48°, 132°, 228°, or 312°
$$\csc\theta=\pm\sqrt{\frac{9.5-2.3}{4}}=\pm\sqrt{1.8}\approx\pm1.34.$$
$$\theta=\csc^{-1}(\pm1.34)\approx\sin^{-1}(\pm0.75).$$

5. 110° or 290°
$$\tan\theta=\frac{-17+3}{9-4}=-\frac{14}{5}.\ \theta=\tan^{-1}\left(-\frac{14}{5}\right).$$

6. 55°, 125°, 235°, or 305°
$$\sec\theta=\pm\sqrt{\frac{49}{16}}=\pm\frac{7}{4}.$$
$$\theta=\sec^{-1}\left(\pm\frac{7}{4}\right)=\cos^{-1}\left(\pm\frac{4}{7}\right).$$

7. 0°, 18°, 180°, or 198°
Factor as $(\tan\theta)(3\tan\theta-1)=0$.
$$\theta=\tan^{-1}(0)\text{ or }\theta=\tan^{-1}\left(\frac{1}{3}\right).$$

8. 90°, 226°, or 314°
Factor as $(7\sin\theta+5)(\sin\theta-1)=0$.
$$\theta=\sin^{-1}\left(-\frac{5}{7}\right)\text{ or }\theta=\sin^{-1}(1).$$

9. 9°, 27°, 189°, or 207°
Factor as $(\cot\theta-6)(\cot\theta-2)=0$.
$$\theta=\cot^{-1}(6)=\tan^{-1}\left(\frac{1}{6}\right)\text{ or }\theta=\cot^{-1}(2)=\tan^{-1}\left(\frac{1}{2}\right).$$

10. 114° or 246°
Factor as $(5\cos\theta+2)(\cos\theta+3)=0$.
$$\theta=\cos^{-1}\left(-\frac{2}{5}\right)\text{ or }\theta=\cos^{-1}(-3).$$
However, $\cos^{-1}(-3)$ does not exist.

Lessons

14

1. 0°, 104°, 180°, or 256°

Rewrite as $4 \sin \theta + \dfrac{\sin \theta}{\cos \theta} = 0$.

Then $4 \sin \theta \cos \theta + \sin \theta = 0$.
Factor as $(\sin \theta)(4 \cos \theta + 1) = 0$.

$\theta = \sin^{-1}(0)$ or $\theta = \cos^{-1}\left(-\dfrac{1}{4}\right)$.

2. 37°, 143°, 217°, or 323°

Rewrite as $25 \sin \theta - \dfrac{9}{\sin \theta} = 0$.

Then $25 \sin^2 \theta - 9 = 0$.
Factor as $(5 \sin \theta - 3)(5 \sin \theta + 3) = 0$.

$\theta = \sin^{-1}\left(\dfrac{3}{5}\right)$ or $\theta = \sin^{-1}\left(-\dfrac{3}{5}\right)$.

3. 90° or 270°

Rewrite as $3 \cos \theta - \dfrac{7 \cos \theta}{\sin \theta} = 0$.

Then $3 \cos \theta \sin \theta - 7 \cos \theta = 0$.
Factor as $(\cos \theta)(3 \sin \theta - 7) = 0$.

$\theta = \cos^{-1}(0)$ or $\theta = \sin^{-1}\left(\dfrac{7}{3}\right)$.

However, $\sin^{-1}\left(\dfrac{7}{3}\right)$ does not exist.

4. 19°, 161°, 199°, or 341°

Rewrite as $8 \tan \theta - \cot \theta = 0$,

which becomes $8 \tan \theta - \dfrac{1}{\tan \theta} = 0$.

Then $8 \tan^2 \theta - 1 = 0$. $\tan \theta = \pm\sqrt{\dfrac{1}{8}} \approx \pm 0.3536$.

$\theta = \tan^{-1}(0.3536)$ or $\theta = \tan^{-1}(-0.3536)$.

5. 12° or 168°

Using $\sin^2 \theta + \cos^2 \theta = 1$,
rewrite as $1 - 5 \sin \theta = 0$.

Thus, $\theta = \sin^{-1}\left(\dfrac{1}{5}\right)$.

14
(cont.)

6. 116° or 244°

Rewrite as $(4)(\sin^2 \theta + \cos^2 \theta) + 9 \cos \theta = 0$, which becomes $4 + 9 \cos \theta = 0$.

$\theta = \cos^{-1}\left(-\dfrac{4}{9}\right)$.

7. 190° or 350°

Using $\cot^2 \theta + 1 = \csc^2 \theta$, rewrite as $\csc^2 \theta + 6 \csc \theta = 0$.
Factor as $(\csc \theta)(\csc \theta + 6) = 0$.

$\theta = \csc^{-1}(0)$ or $\theta = \csc^{-1}(-6) = \sin^{-1}\left(-\dfrac{1}{6}\right)$.

However, $\csc^{-1}(0)$ does not exist.

8. 49°, 131°, 210°, or 330°

Since $\cot^2 \theta = \csc^2 \theta - 1$, rewrite as $(3)(\csc^2 \theta - 1) + 2 \csc \theta - 5 = 0$, which becomes $3 \csc^2 \theta + 2 \csc \theta - 8 = 0$.
Factor as $(3 \csc \theta - 4)(\csc \theta + 2) = 0$.

$\theta = \csc^{-1}\left(\dfrac{4}{3}\right) = \sin^{-1}\left(\dfrac{3}{4}\right)$ or

$\theta = \csc^{-1}(-2) = \sin^{-1}\left(-\dfrac{1}{2}\right)$.

9. 96°, 180°, or 264°

Since $\tan^2 \theta = \sec^2 \theta - 1$, rewrite as $\sec^2 \theta - 1 + 10 \sec \theta + 10 = 0$, which becomes $\sec^2 \theta + 10 \sec \theta + 9 = 0$.
Factor as $(\sec \theta + 1)(\sec \theta + 9) = 0$.
$\theta = \sec^{-1}(-1) = \cos^{-1}(-1)$ or

$\theta = \sec^{-1}(-9) = \cos^{-1}\left(-\dfrac{1}{9}\right)$.

10. 58°, 117°, 238°, or 297°

Using $\tan^2 \theta + 1 = \sec^2 \theta$, rewrite as $(5)(\tan^2 \theta + 1) + 2 \tan \theta - 21 = 0$, which becomes $5 \tan^2 \theta + 2 \tan \theta - 16 = 0$.
Factor as $(5 \tan \theta - 8)(\tan \theta + 2) = 0$.

$\theta = \tan^{-1}\left(\dfrac{8}{5}\right)$ or $\theta = \tan^{-1}(-2)$.

Lessons

15

1. 77° or 167°

$3 \tan(2\theta) = -1.5.$

$2\theta = \tan^{-1}\left(-\dfrac{1.5}{3}\right) \approx 153.4°$ or $333.4°$.

$\theta = \left(\dfrac{1}{2}\right)(153.4°)$ or $\theta = \left(\dfrac{1}{2}\right)(333.4°)$.

2. 32° or 148°

$\sec(2\theta) = 6.5 - 4.3 = 2.2.$
$2\theta = \sec^{-1}(2.2) \approx \cos^{-1}(0.45) \approx 63.3°$ or $296.7°$.

$\theta = \left(\dfrac{1}{2}\right)(63.3°)$ or $\theta = \left(\dfrac{1}{2}\right)(296.7°)$.

3. 100° or 170°

$\sin 2\theta = \dfrac{-8.4 + 5}{10} = -0.34.$
$2\theta = \sin^{-1}(-0.34) \approx 199.9°$ or $340.1°$.

$\theta = \left(\dfrac{1}{2}\right)(199.9°)$ or $\theta = \left(\dfrac{1}{2}\right)(340.1°)$.

4. 9° or 99°

Rewrite as $8 \cot 2\theta - 3 = 5 \cot 2\theta + 6$,
which becomes $3 \cot 2\theta = 9$.

$2\theta = \cot^{-1}(3) = \tan^{-1}\left(\dfrac{1}{3}\right) \approx 18.4°$ or $198.4°$.

$\theta = \left(\dfrac{1}{2}\right)(18.4°)$ or $\theta = \left(\dfrac{1}{2}\right)(198.4°)$.

5. 4°, 86°, 105°, or 165°

Factor as $(\csc 2\theta - 7)(\csc 2\theta + 2)$.

$2\theta = \csc^{-1}(7) = \sin^{-1}\left(\dfrac{1}{7}\right) \approx 8.2°$ or $171.8°$.

$2\theta = \csc^{-1}(-2) = \sin^{-1}\left(-\dfrac{1}{2}\right) = 210°$ or $330°$.

$\theta = \left(\dfrac{1}{2}\right)(8.2°)$, $\theta = \left(\dfrac{1}{2}\right)(171.8°)$,

$\theta = \left(\dfrac{1}{2}\right)(210°)$, or $\theta = \left(\dfrac{1}{2}\right)(330°)$.

Lessons

6. 90°, 217°, 270°, or 323°

Rewrite as $6 \cos \theta + (5)(2 \sin \theta \cos \theta) = 0$.
Factor as $(2 \cos \theta)(3 + 5 \sin \theta) = 0$.

$\theta = \cos^{-1}(0)$ or $\theta = \sin^{-1}\left(-\dfrac{3}{5}\right)$.

7. 0°, 68°, 180°, or 292°

Rewrite as $(4)(2 \sin \theta \cos \theta) - 3 \sin \theta = 0$.
Factor as $(\sin \theta)(8 \cos \theta - 3) = 0$.

$\theta = \sin^{-1}(0)$ or $\theta = \cos^{-1}\left(\dfrac{3}{8}\right)$.

8. 16°, 17°, 106°, or 107°

Factor as $(3 \cot 2\theta - 5)(2 \cot 2\theta - 3) = 0$.

$2\theta = \cot^{-1}\left(\dfrac{5}{3}\right) = \tan^{-1}\left(\dfrac{3}{5}\right) \approx 31°$ or $211°$.

$2\theta = \cot^{-1}\left(\dfrac{3}{2}\right) = \tan^{-1}\left(\dfrac{2}{3}\right) \approx 33.7°$ or $213.7°$.

$\theta = \left(\dfrac{1}{2}\right)(31°), \theta = \left(\dfrac{1}{2}\right)(33.7°).$

$\theta = \left(\dfrac{1}{2}\right)(211°),$ or $\theta = \left(\dfrac{1}{2}\right)(213.7°).$

9. 120° or 240°

Since $\cos 2\theta = 2 \cos^2 \theta - 1$,
rewrite as $(4)(2 \cos^2 \theta - 1) - 6 \cos \theta - 1 = 0$,
which becomes $8 \cos^2 \theta - 6 \cos \theta - 5 = 0$.
Factor as $(4 \cos \theta - 5)(2 \cos \theta + 1) = 0$.

$\theta = \cos^{-1}\left(\dfrac{5}{4}\right)$ or $\theta = \cos^{-1}\left(-\dfrac{1}{2}\right)$.

However, $\cos^{-1}\left(\dfrac{5}{4}\right)$ does not exist.

10. 19°, 161°, 199°, or 341°

Since $\cos 2\theta = 1 - 2 \sin^2 \theta$,
rewrite as $(2)(1 - 2 \sin^2 \theta) + 13 \sin^2 \theta - 3 = 0$.
Then $2 - 4 \sin^2 \theta + 13 \sin^2 \theta - 3 = 0$,
which becomes $9 \sin^2 \theta - 1 = 0$.
Factor as $(3 \sin \theta - 1)(3 \sin \theta + 1) = 0$.

$\theta = \sin^{-1}\left(\dfrac{1}{3}\right)$ or $\theta = \sin^{-1}\left(-\dfrac{1}{3}\right)$.

Quizzes

1

1. D   Sine θ = Opposite side divided by hypotenuse = $4 \div 5$.

2. B   For any fourth quadrant angle θ, tan θ = –tan(360° – θ). For example, tan 300° = – tan 60° $\approx$ –1.73.

3. A   90° is equivalent to $(90)\left(\dfrac{\pi}{180}\right)$ radians.

4. C   In moving from 4 to 9, the number of degrees through which the minute hand rotates is $(360°)\left(\dfrac{5}{12}\right)$.

5. B   Definitions of standard position and positive measurement of an angle.

6. C   Since $\cot \theta = \dfrac{\cos \theta}{\sin \theta}$, cos θ = (cot θ)(sin θ) = (–2.5)(0.37).

7. D   The reference angle for any third quadrant angle θ is θ – 180°.

8. D $\sin 57° = \dfrac{RN}{19}$, so $RN \approx$ (19)(0.8387).

9. A   If sin θ = –1, then θ = 270° only. For each of answer choices (B), (C), and (D), there are two values of θ. For example, in answer choice (B), a correct value of θ is found in the first and fourth quadrants.

10. B $\cos 23° = \dfrac{36}{OA}$, so $OA \approx \dfrac{36}{0.9205}$.

2

1. C   Whenever $\theta < 90°$, $\cos \theta = \sin(90° - \theta)$.
For example, $\cos 40° = \sin 50° \approx 0.7660$.

2. A   Point J may be located anywhere along $\overline{GK}$, so we cannot compare the sizes of GJ and JK.

3. D $b = \sqrt{10^2 - 5.4^2} = \sqrt{70.84}$.

4. C $\tan^{-1}(0.543) \approx 29°$ or $209°$. Choose the larger angle value.

5. B $\sec^{-1}(-2.6) \approx \cos^{-1}(-0.3846)$. Select the second quadrant value.

6. C $\tan 50° = \dfrac{PQ}{8}$, so $PQ \approx (8)(1.1918) \approx 9.53$.

Then $PS = \sqrt{20^2 + 9.53^2} = \sqrt{490.82}$.

7. A $\csc \pi = \dfrac{1}{\sin \pi} = \dfrac{1}{0}$.

8. C $\cos 215° = -\cos 35° = -\sin 55° = \sin(180° + 55°)$.

9. A   Angle of elevation $= \sin^{-1}\left(\dfrac{40}{75}\right)$.

10. B $\sin 34° = \dfrac{DC}{20}$, so $DC \approx (20)(0.5592) \approx 11.18$.

Since $\tan 18° = \dfrac{11.18}{FC}$, $FC \approx \dfrac{11.18}{0.3249}$.

Quizzes

3

1. C $\quad \dfrac{15}{\sin 80°} = \dfrac{b}{\sin 42°}$, so $b \approx \dfrac{(15)(0.6691)}{0.9848}$.

2. D $\quad \dfrac{45}{\sin 65°} = \dfrac{26}{\sin \angle B}$. $\angle B \approx \sin^{-1}\left(\dfrac{(26)(0.9063)}{45}\right) \approx \sin^{-1}(0.5236)$.

3. C $\quad \cos 72° = \dfrac{WZ}{25}$, so $WZ \approx (25)(0.3090) = 7.725$. Also, $\sin 72° = \dfrac{ZY}{25}$.
Thus, $ZY \approx (25)(0.9511) = 23.778$. Finally, $7.725 + 23.778$.

4. B $\quad GJ^2 = 18^2 + 27^2 - (2)(18)(27)(\cos 74°) \approx 785.08$. Then $GJ = \sqrt{785.08}$.

5. C $\quad HJ^2 = 6^2 + 24^2 - (2)(6)(24)(\cos 100°) \approx 662.01$. So $HJ = \sqrt{662.01} \approx 25.73$.
Then $\dfrac{25.73}{\sin 100°} = \dfrac{6}{\sin \angle J}$. Thus, $\angle J \approx \sin^{-1}\left(\dfrac{(6)(0.9848)}{25.73}\right) \approx \sin^{-1}(0.2296)$.

6. B $\quad KN = NM = 66$. Then $66^2 = 66^2 + 80^2 - (2)(66)(80)(\cos \angle KMN)$.
$-6400 = (-10,560)(\cos \angle KMN)$, so $\angle KMN = \cos^{-1}(0.6061)$.

7. D $\quad$ Since $\angle P = 180° - 105° - 29° = 46°$, $\dfrac{PQ}{\sin 105°} = \dfrac{52}{\sin 46°}$.
Then $PQ \approx \dfrac{(52)(0.9659)}{0.7193}$.

8. C $\quad 42^2 = 36^2 + 23^2 - (2)(36)(23)(\cos \angle T)$.
$-61 = (-1656)(\cos \angle T)$, so $\angle T \approx \cos^{-1}(0.0368) \approx 88°$.
Thus, $\angle WVT = 180° - 88°$.

9. A $\quad$ Since $\angle BDH = 180° - 140° - 24° = 16°$, $\dfrac{DH}{\sin 140°} = \dfrac{33}{\sin 16°}$.
Then $DH \approx \dfrac{(33)(0.6428)}{0.2756}$.

10. A $\quad$ Semi-perimeter $= (8 + 11 + 15) \div 2 = 17$.
Area $= \sqrt{(17)(9)(6)(2)} = \sqrt{1836}$.

4

1. B   Rewrite as $\dfrac{4}{\tan\theta} - \dfrac{\tan\theta}{3} = 0$.

Multiply by $3\tan\theta$ and rearrange terms to get $\tan^2\theta = 12$.
Then $\theta = \pm\tan^{-1}(\sqrt{12}) \approx \pm\tan^{-1}(3.4641)$.

2. B   Factor as $(\sec\theta - 8)(\sec\theta + 1) = 0$.

Then $\theta = \sec^{-1}(8) = \cos^{-1}\left(\dfrac{1}{8}\right)$ or $\theta = \sec^{-1}(-1) = \cos^{-1}(-1)$.

3. A   Rewrite as $(2)(2\cos^2\theta - 1) + 5\cos\theta - 4 = 0$.
Simplify to $4\cos^2\theta + 5\cos\theta - 6 = 0$.
Factor as $(4\cos\theta - 3)(\cos\theta + 2) = 0$.

$\theta = \cos^{-1}\left(\dfrac{3}{4}\right)$ or $\theta = \cos^{-1}(-2)$.

However, $\cos^{-1}(-2)$ does not exist.

4. C   Subtract 6.3, then divide by 2 to get $\csc\theta = -3.9$.
Then $\theta = \csc^{-1}(-3.9) \approx \sin^{-1}(-0.2564)$.

5. B   Factor as $(\tan\theta)(4\tan\theta + 1) = 0$.

$\theta = \tan^{-1}(0)$ or $\theta = \tan^{-1}\left(-\dfrac{1}{4}\right)$.

6. C   Using the identity $\sin^2\theta + \cos^2\theta = 1$,

rewrite as $(3)(1) - 7\cos\theta = 0$. Then $\theta = \cos^{-1}\left(\dfrac{3}{7}\right)$.

Quizzes

4
(cont.)

7. D   Combine similar terms and rearrange to get $2.5 \csc 2\theta = 3$.
Then $2\theta = \csc^{-1}\left(\dfrac{3}{2.5}\right) = \sin^{-1}\left(\dfrac{2.5}{3}\right)$
$\approx \sin^{-1}(0.8333) \approx 56.4°$ or $123.6°$.
Finally, $\theta = \left(\dfrac{1}{2}\right)(56.4°)$ or $\theta = \left(\dfrac{1}{2}\right)(123.6°)$.

8. B   Using the identity $\tan^2 \theta = \sec^2 \theta - 1$,
rewrite as $(6)(\sec^2 \theta - 1) + 13 \sec \theta + 1 = 0$.
Simplify to $6 \sec^2 \theta + 13 \sec \theta - 5 = 0$.
Factor as $(3 \sec \theta - 1)(2 \sec \theta + 5) = 0$.
$\theta = \sec^{-1}\left(\dfrac{1}{3}\right) = \cos^{-1}(3)$ or $\theta = \sec^{-1}\left(-\dfrac{5}{2}\right) = \cos^{-1}\left(-\dfrac{2}{5}\right)$.
However, $\cos^{-1}(3)$ does not exist.

9. D   Using the identity $\csc^2 \theta = \cot^2 \theta + 1$,
rewrite as $(2)(\cot^2 \theta + 1) + 7 \cot \theta - 2 = 0$.
Simplify to $2 \cot^2 \theta + 7 \cot \theta = 0$.
Factor as $(\cot \theta)(2 \cot \theta + 7) = 0$.
$\theta = \cot^{-1}(0)$ or $\theta = \cot^{-1}\left(-\dfrac{7}{2}\right) = \tan^{-1}\left(-\dfrac{2}{7}\right)$.

10. A   Factor as $(10 \cos \theta - 3)(10 \cos \theta + 3) = 0$.
$\theta = \cos^{-1}\left(\dfrac{3}{10}\right)$ or $\theta = \cos^{-1}\left(-\dfrac{3}{10}\right)$.

1. **C**   Factor as (cos θ)(3 cos θ + 4) = 0.

Then $\theta = \cos^{-1}(0)$ or $\theta = \cos^{-1}\left(-\dfrac{4}{3}\right)$.

However, $\cos^{-1}\left(-\dfrac{4}{3}\right)$ does not exist.
(Trigonometric Equations)

2. **C**   Rewrite as 9 cot 2θ = 2 cot 2θ – 6. Then 7 cot 2θ = –6,

so $2\theta = \cot^{-1}\left(-\dfrac{6}{7}\right) = \tan^{-1}\left(-\dfrac{7}{6}\right) \approx 130.6°$ or $310.6°$.

Thus, $\theta = \dfrac{130.6°}{2}$ or $\theta = \dfrac{310.6°}{2}$.
(Trigonometric Equations)

3. **B**   Regardless of the quadrant in which θ is located, $\cot\theta = \dfrac{1}{\tan\theta}$.

Since $\tan\theta = \dfrac{3}{11}$, $\cot\theta = \dfrac{1}{\frac{3}{11}}$.
(Trigonometric Ratios)

4. **B**   Whenever $\pi < \theta < \dfrac{3\pi}{2}$, where θ is measured in radians,

cos θ = –cos(θ – π).
(Trigonometric Ratios)

5. **A**   Definitions of standard position and quadrantal angle.
(Angle Measurement)

6. **B**   After 4 hours, their distances are 18 miles and 14.4 miles.
Then the distance between them is $\sqrt{18^2 + 14.4^2} = \sqrt{531.36}$ miles.
(Pythagorean theorem)

7. **A** $VX^2 = 32^2 + 21^2 - (2)(32)(21)(\cos 104°) \approx 1790.14$.
Then $VX = \sqrt{1790.14}$.
(Law of Cosines)

8. **C**   Rewrite as 8 cos θ + (7)(2 sin θ cos θ) = 0.

Factor as (2 cos θ)(4 + 7 sin θ) = 0.

$\theta = \cos^{-1}(0)$ or $\theta = \sin^{-1}\left(-\dfrac{4}{7}\right)$.
(Trigonometric Equations)

Cumulative Exam

9. A $\angle B = 180° - 32° - 64° = 84°$.

$\dfrac{EH}{\sin 84°} = \dfrac{15}{\sin 32°}$, so $EH = \dfrac{(15)(\sin 84°)}{\sin 32°}$.
(Law of Sines)

10. D   2 radians $= (2)\left(\dfrac{180}{\pi}\right) \approx 115°$. Each of the 12 numbers on

a clock is separated by $\dfrac{360}{12} = 30°$. Since $\dfrac{115}{30} \approx 3.8$, the

minute hand will point to four numbers after 12.
(Radian Measurement)

11. C $\theta = \cos^{-1}\left(\dfrac{33}{44}\right)$.

(Word Problem Applications)

12. B $1 : \sqrt{3} : 2$ Right triangle. Then $\cot 60° = \tan 30° = \dfrac{1}{\sqrt{3}}$.

(Special Right Triangles)

13. D $\dfrac{28}{\sin \angle R} = \dfrac{15}{\sin 25°}$. $\sin \angle R = \dfrac{(28)(\sin 25°)}{15} \approx 0.7889$.

$\angle R = \sin^{-1}(0.7889) \approx 128°$, since $\angle R$ is obtuse.
Then $\angle T = 180° - 25° - 128°$. (Law of Sines)

14. A   If $\csc \theta + 2.5 = 3.3$, then $\csc \theta = 0.8$.
However, $\csc \theta$ must be either at least 1 or at most -1.
(Trigonometric Ratios)

15. A   Rewrite as $\dfrac{5}{\tan \theta} - \dfrac{\tan \theta}{2} = 0$.

Multiply by 2 tan θ to get $10 - \tan^2 \theta = 0$.
Then $\tan \theta = \pm\sqrt{10} \approx \pm 3.16$, so $\theta = \tan^{-1}(\pm 3.16)$.
(Trigonometric Equations)

16. D   Semi-perimeter is $(10 + 13 + 17) \div 2 = 20$.
Area $= \sqrt{(20)(10)(7)(3)} = \sqrt{4200}$.
(Heron's Formula)

17. D   Angle of depression = angle of elevation.
Let x = height of cliff.

Then $\tan 16° = \dfrac{x}{550}$. so $x = (550)(\tan 16°)$.

(Word Problem Applications)

18. A Rewrite as $(9)(\sin^2\theta + \cos^2\theta) + 16\cos\theta = 0$.
Since $\sin^2\theta + \cos^2\theta = 1$, the equation becomes $9 + 16\cos\theta = 0$.
Then $\cos\theta = -\dfrac{9}{16}$, so $\theta = \cos^{-1}\left(-\dfrac{9}{16}\right)$.
(Trigonometric Equations)

19. B $\tan 15° = \dfrac{HK}{68}$, so $HK = (68)(\tan 15°) \approx 18.22$.

Then $\sin 70° = \dfrac{18.22}{HL}$. Thus, $HL = \dfrac{18.22}{\sin 70°}$.
(Overlapping Right Triangles)

20. A $\tan 28° = \dfrac{MQ}{21}$, so $MQ = (21)(\tan 28°) \approx 11.17$.

Then $\angle N = \tan^{-1}\left(\dfrac{11.17}{12}\right) \approx \tan^{-1}(0.9308)$.
(Adjacent Right Triangles)

21. B Each of (A), (C), and (D) is equivalent to stating that the
secant of a 180°-angle is –1 . Answer choice (B) states that
the secant of a 1°-angle is 180. (This is also false since sec 1° ≈ 1).
(Trigonometric Ratios)

22. C In $\triangle QRS$, RS is also 18. $14^2 = 18^2 + 18^2 - (2)(18)(18)(\cos \angle R)$.
Then $196 = 324 + 324 - (648)(\cos \angle R)$,
which becomes $-452 = (-648)(\cos \angle R)$.
Thus, $\angle R = \cos^{-1}\left(\dfrac{452}{648}\right) \approx \cos^{-1}(0.6975)$.
(Law of Cosines)

23. C Using the identity $\tan^2\theta + 1 = \sec^2\theta$, $\tan^2\theta + 1 = 2.4025$.
Then $\tan^2\theta = 1.4025$.
Since θ is in the second quadrant, $\tan\theta$ must be negative.
Thus, $\tan\theta = -\sqrt{1.4025}$.
(Trigonometric Identities)

24. D $ZY = 27 - 17 = 10$, so $\tan \angle WYZ = \dfrac{15}{10} = 1.5$.

$\angle WYZ = \tan^{-1}(1.5) \approx 56°$.
Thus, $\angle WYX = 180° - 56°$.
(Overlapping Right Triangles)

25. B In $\triangle ADG$, let $x = AG$.
Then $\cos 77° = \dfrac{7}{x}$, so, $x = \dfrac{7}{\cos 77°}$.
(Trigonometric Ratios)

Workspace

Workspace

Workspace

Workspace

SCORECARD
Trigonometry

Lesson	Completed	Number of Drill Questions	Number Correct	What I need to review...
1		10		
2		10		
3		10		
4		10		
5		10		
6		10		
7		10		
8		10		
9		10		
10		10		
11		10		
12		10		
13		10		
14		10		
15		10		

Quiz		What I need to review...
1	/10	
2	/10	
3	/10	
4	/10	

Cumulative Exam	/25	